THE
POSITIVE
EFFECT

A RETAIL LEADER'S GUIDE TO
CHANGING THE WORLD

APRIL SABRAL

BALBOA.PRESS

A DIVISION OF HAY HOUSE

Balboa Press books may be ordered through booksellers or by contacting:

Balboa Press
A Division of Hay House
1663 Liberty Drive
Bloomington, IN 47403
www.balboapress.com
844-682-1282

Cover Design: Amber Joy
Cover Photo: Josie Cipriano

Print information available on the last page.

ISBN: 978-1-9822-7889-2 (sc)
ISBN: 978-1-9822-7891-5 (hc)
ISBN: 978-1-9822-7890-8 (e)

Library of Congress Control Number: 2022900929

Balboa Press rev. date: 05/05/2022

CONTENTS

A PERSONAL NOTE FROM APRIL

This book is a result of a journey to find self-love and how I found it through my journey in retail.

I have struggled my entire life with self-esteem—what others see as a confident, assured mum and businesswoman is not the person I saw when I looked in the mirror.

Growing up, I was socially awkward and extremely shy. I had an extreme lisp, which was paralyzing. My early years did not help me grow into a confident young woman—as a teen, I became very self-conscious when talking in front of people. Lucky for me, I had an extremely outgoing twin sister who could talk to everyone, so I didn't really have to. I could hide behind her personality and popularity.

My self-worth was slowly eroded over time, and because of this, I made terrible choices when it came to emotional relationships in my personal life. My lack of self-esteem has plagued me for as long as I can remember. Today, it is still an ongoing battle, and I think it will always be something that I am aware of and working on. The need for approval decreases as I age, for which I am grateful.

My lack of self-worth was amplified by many events that occurred early in my life:

1. The separation of my parents when I was four.
2. When I was eight years old, I went to boarding school, which had a profound effect on me, one that left me feeling unloved and rejected.
3. A twin sister who I thought was prettier, more popular, and smarter than me.

Growing up as a twin, I was constantly compared to my sister. If I didn't get grades as high as hers, I was viewed as if there was something wrong with me. This lack of self-value was reinforced as I grew from a teenager into a young adult. My relationship with my sister became more and more distant, and I always felt she didn't feel the need to have a close relationship with me, unlike what I imagined about most twins. I thought she did not see me as someone of value in her life. This continued into my adult life.

I think many of us struggle with these kinds of feelings, even if we do not want to admit it. Not being seen or valued is soul-destroying; it robs you of your confidence, keeps you in fear, and pushes you into a corner, convincing you to play small in life. I know because this was me for a very long time.

I knew I was different. What I didn't know was why I was different. I didn't realize that my particular brand of different was a signal that I was uniquely crafted and destined to make an impact on the world.

I felt I didn't fit in, and the experiences I created (yes, I do mean created) in my life were because I didn't know who I was. I didn't value my gifts, and I reinforced my uncertainty by allowing people in my private life to treat me as weak throughout my earlier years.

Now that I am in my forties and have the benefit of life lessons learned, I pay attention to what amplifies or triggers those sensations of self-worth, whereas, in my twenties, they were just who I was. In my thirties, I was learning and studying how to change my mindset and love myself. Now, in my forties, I have learned how to overcome it. Although I am by no means a master of self-love yet (none of us are), I am acutely aware that self-love is my greatest life lesson to master and probably always will be.

My life had been a series of events that happened to me and not something I thought I consciously chose. Going to boarding school at age eight was not my choice, dropping out of college was not my choice, moving out of my home at sixteen was not my choice, and landing my first job in a retail store was not my first choice.

Back then, I always felt my life was happening to me and that I just didn't have the smarts, the confidence, or the money to choose the kind of life I dreamed about having: a great husband, perfect home, and a career people respected. I longed for a family who supported me and grandparents and cousins that I saw all the time. I craved a high school experience like the ones you see on the TV shows.

I would consider myself back then a passive bystander; I was someone who let life happen to me.

I felt like life was thrown at me and that I had to just suck it up and accept it. Lucky for me, deep down, I am an overly optimistic dreamer, which kept me in my head a lot of the time, dreaming about what life could be like versus what life was.

The first "taking control" moment in my life happened when I was twenty-three. It was the day I found out I was pregnant with my daughter. Her dad and I were in love and worked together in a store in central London—Oxford Street area. We had become best friends working in a very well-known independent Italian designer boutique and had not planned on having a family or settling down.

I remember making the decision that I was going to have my baby and thinking that no matter what happened, I was choosing to bring this little person into the world.

I was nervous, and so was he! But we decided we were going to have our baby. This was a turning point in my life. At twenty-three, I was going to be responsible for another human being. I would have someone to love and look after. This paradigm shift had a profound impact on me.

I realized I was going to have to earn more money, work harder, and get better at what I already knew. I wanted to buy my first home, which I did to create a better life for my daughter. When my daughter was three months old, I went back to work, and not long after this, sadly, her father and I decided to split.

I was now a single mum. If I was going to get somewhere in terms of salary and career growth, I needed to work in a larger company with a brand that could help me grow and give me stability.

In the late '90s, The Gap was opening quite a few stores in the UK. I applied for a store manager job, thinking I was sure to get it, as I had been working in retail for nearly six years at that point. I had managed three small boutiques as an area manager for a privately owned Italian chain. Before that, I worked as a sales associate at Paul Smith and Office Shoes, which were two great brands in the UK. I felt confident that with that kind of experience, I would land this new job.

I went to a group interview and was called back into the room. At the end of it, I was offered a merchandising manager position at the Regent Street location, and I accepted it enthusiastically. This was the start of my new life. The rest is history and in this book!

This book is not just about retail. It's much more than that. It's a book about what I have learned in life and how I succeeded in retail, because working in retail is my life.

Thank you to Angee Costa. I never thought I could write a book, but you helped me bring it to life. You are the ideal partner for people who have always wanted to write a book but don't know where to start. You are awesome. Thank you to my talented and creative daughter,

Amber Joy, for designing the cover. Thank you to all my friends for the journey. To all of you who have volunteered your hours, your voices, and supported us as we built retailu.ca—you know who you are—I thank you. We could not have done this without you. As for the journey ahead, I am excited!

Thank you to all of the amazing people who have been part of my journey so far, from the part-timers who chose to work on my team to my immediate direct reports, whom I had the honor of leading, to the peers along the way, my leaders who took risks and gave me the right opportunities, and to the recruiters who found me and opened doors for me. You have all given me something invaluable: support, encouragement, love, energy, parenting advice, food, opportunities, trust, and most of all, the sense of feeling valued and seen.

Each of you has helped me learn to love who I am and who I am still becoming. For this, I am forever grateful.

INTRODUCTION

Books about leadership and retail management are incredibly beneficial and informative. They often point out the many pitfalls leaders encounter and address ways to solve important problems. Is it possible that the issue of leadership, and specifically retail management, can be approached from a completely different angle?

It's easy to forget that retail really means people. Although companies highlight the services and products they offer, the real value behind those products and services are the people who deliver them. In retail, we have the privilege of working alongside people with their myriad personalities, talents, joys, sorrows, experiences, and knowledge. Though we throw around terms like "synergy," "upskilling," and "strategic growth," the real secret to the success of any business is simply the value we place on the people who make it work. Strategic growth means "people growth."

Retail positions are often the first jobs young people have. It is where employees learn many of the life skills needed for career success: working with others, showing up on time, dressing for success, resolving conflict, communication skills, etc. Therefore, retail managers have a golden opportunity to mentor their employees and get them started on a path toward success in their lives by providing positive leadership. When the people in a company are valued and empowered, there is no limit to the heights the company can achieve. This book will share with you tips and best practices you can use to improve your leadership influence and help you have the kinds of conversations your employees will thrive on.

It just takes a commitment on your part to read to the end, follow the guidelines, and make some small but powerful changes on your path toward increased personal development. If you're passionate about self-development and leadership, I am happy to support you in acquiring those mission-critical skills. Just make sure you read the entire book.

Most people struggle with finding purpose and end up in jobs that are less than satisfying. Or they pursue the professions their family members think are best for them. Or, worse, they end up in an industry wholly unsuited for them, where they labor away for thousands of hours every year under the soul-crushing weight of it.

I started my journey in a retail store, part-time at the tender age of sixteen. Honestly, I just needed a way to pay my rent and figure out what I wanted to do with my life. Sometimes life has a way of steering you right where you belong, even if it's not the place you think you're supposed to be. Retail, for me, was a means to an end to pay bills. It was easy to get hired, as no formal education was required. For many years, I thought of it as "just a job." Looking back, my retail journey helped me discover the purpose of my life. Little did I know that developing people through coaching them, and building world class customer-focused teams that strived to make every buyer's experience exceptional, would become my daily norm. I continued to study leadership and learn from mentors who took me under their wings. I learned about people and what it meant to manage and shoulder all of the responsibilities I was given.

As I delved into self-development books and seminars about how to be a more effective leader, I realized that my journey to helping others was activating a deep desire to teach leaders how to connect with and value the people working for them.

I learned that building others—whether through coaching, merchandising, or mindset training—was my role and, ultimately, my purpose. Through years of training and developing people in the retail space, I discovered my passion for teaching and mentoring. I unearthed my natural abilities for creating winning cultures and positive environments where conditions are ripe for teams to thrive and grow.

When I started in retail, I was unsure about what to do with my life. Still, as I grew in my various roles and my skills developed, my passion was revealed, and I discovered a desire for facilitating meaningful relationships between people. I believe that this desire to show people how to connect on a deeper level was always inside me. Retail brought it to the surface.

Now that I have left the traditional executive role and started my own company, I understand how each position I have held and each person I have reported to has played a part in helping me evolve into my current function as a trainer and mentor in retail.

There are millions of books and courses available to help people discover their purpose. They are popular because the search for meaning is fundamental to the human experience. Many people find their meaning and identity in their occupation—I know I do.

When I stepped down as vice president, it was a scary decision. I was losing part of my identity and having to craft a new one. I remember being invited to speak at a conference because of my vice president title prior to this decision being made; when this happened, I remember contacting the conference organizers to let them know I was no longer the vice president of DAVIDsTEA, and I found myself feeling nervous about being on stage and speaking. I thought I had lost something. In reality, I had just promoted myself to the CEO of my own company. I continued to be a featured speaker, and it went extremely well. It's funny how our worth is so wrapped up in what we do versus who we are. Think about this for a moment, and ask yourself this question: What would you have felt or done in the same situation?

In working with my retail family, I have discovered my strength, opened doors of opportunities, and, most importantly, solidified my purpose. As a leadership coach, the retail cross-functional lessons are invaluable to my clients. My company is creating courses and seminars that will help leaders and their teams create meaningful work environments.

I feel fortunate to have worked within retail with the amazing customers and employees I have met. Because of my experiences, I recommend that you ask yourself if the job you hold ignites your passions and invigorates your desires. If you can answer yes to that question, you are well on your way to finding your purpose—whatever that may be.

The key to a fulfilling career starts with not seeing your job as just a paycheck. Instead, think about it as a platform to practice and learn. Then use what you have learned to "pay it forward" and teach others. It has been said that you meet your best friends in a retail job. I can confirm that to be true. My best friend was my former boss over twenty-five years ago, and we are both still in retail, although in different capacities.

I don't see myself as a sales leader. I see myself as a people leader. It may sound weird to hear me say that my passion is people. It may even sound vague to you—but not to me. Some people love fashion. Some love design. I love people and seeing them thrive. I have had the pleasure of working with the very best of them for twenty-five years. It has been a thrilling and fulfilling ride.

So, what is my story? I don't see myself as better or different than most people or those I work with; in fact, I see my life as quite normal. Nevertheless, I do appreciate that it is a story just like yours. As I approach my mid-life years (forties, which is the new twenty, BTW), I find more and more people ask me about my life and want to know how a Brit ended up living in Canada. They want to know where I am from and how I got to where I am in my life and career. It seems like the answer is not that straightforward. I have lived in multiple places and countries over the last four decades. I grew up in the UK and with an identical twin sister and two brothers. Both my parents were American. (Despite my name, I was not born in April.)

Mum and Dad moved to the UK in the early '70s, both American hippies. A lot of my childhood was spent traveling around the UK. My mum was an antique dealer, and my dad was the primary caregiver until he left, when I was four, as he could not work legally in the UK. As I said, my mum was an antique dealer and entrepreneur, and I remember often driving around the countryside with a big piece of furniture in the back of our Volvo station wagon. This was the antique dealer's signature car. I can also remember visiting many auction rooms and always being around a selling culture.

Everything in our house had a price sticker on it. Everything was for sale for the right price. Perhaps this is why I'm not attached to material things. It is undoubtedly the reason I have a passion for retail. I grew up watching my mother build relationships with her customers and listening to the stories about each piece of furniture. I love to buy other people's things, which sounds weird; however, when you have lived in a house where everything is on its way to someone else, it teaches you that buying new is not always as exciting or fun.

Those early years and experiences shaped me into the person I am today. We moved many times before I reached the age of six. We lived above an antique shop and spent countless hours trekking around the countryside with my twin sister and my mum, buying and selling pieces of furniture from our car. All of these diverse experiences have helped me as I pursued a career in retail. For example, I mastered the art of peacekeeping with my twin sister after hours in the car with her, which now I would call the art of compromise or conflict avoidance management styles in leadership. As twins, we argued a lot; but we would then move on and forget quickly, which developed my conflict management and cooperation skills.

When we were young, I watched my sister tumble down the stairs headfirst. I thought she was bold and an adventurer. I developed the skill of learning from observing her to minimize my own mistakes. I would turn around slowly and shuffle down backward to not repeat hurting myself, unlike my sister, who went before me. This is just one simple situation, but it is a very practical example. These kinds of lessons taught me to learn from others and not always to think I know best. When people have gone before you, they have valuable life experience. There were many more life lessons. It seems I was always looking at small events in life and learning big lessons from them. When I began my career in retail, I made it my mission to seek out others who had been successful in a particular field and convince them to teach me their successes.

At the tender age of sixteen, I wasn't getting on with my new stepfather, so I moved out of the family home. I had to get a job immediately to survive. The easiest job to get at that age was in a retail store, as I didn't need a degree or certificate of education. All I needed to do was to show up on time, look decent, and help customers. My first job was in a small boutique in Manchester, where I learned to sell menswear.

After a few years, I moved to London and worked for a few different retailers, one of them being the designer, Paul Smith. I remember meeting this retail fashion icon at the store in Covent Garden when I got my first suit fitting. Yes, I met Paul Smith when I was a late teen. I also worked for Gap and met the company's founders, the Fishers, during a store visit in the Marble Arch location. I worked for Starbucks and met Howard Schultz while he visited my store. At the time, I didn't think much of it, but now looking back, meeting such iconic retail legends in my early years inspired me to work harder and dedicate myself to their brands. After meeting Howard at a press conference held at my store, I bought my first leadership book, called *Pour Your Heart into It*. This inspired me to do my best every day and make a difference. I loved his story and the real struggle he endured to start such a great business.

While my story may seem unusual to some, the truth is we all have a story to tell. And the experiences we have been through are the tools that will assist us in helping others today. As I was living through my strange life, it all felt quite normal to me. I was simply doing what I had to so that I could fit in and survive. My upbringing prepared me for the life I live today. I count every tragedy and triumph as a blessing and value what they added to my existence.

Though I am a teacher of retail leadership skills, I am forever the student open to learning from others. People often ask me what I do. I sometimes find it hard to put into words. My answer varies because my role is forever evolving. I'm a consultant. I'm a leadership coach. I'm an operations specialist. And now I'm an author. But the elevator pitch is this: I build people. Developing a culture where people are free to explore, attempt, fail, and succeed is a good idea for any organization. But the million-dollar question is the *how*. What makes some leaders great and some even greater? What is it in leadership that enables a culture of growth and development?

I work with lots of leaders who are constantly reading and learning about leadership. However, not all of them act on what they learn. Then there are others who read nothing but still naturally lead. When you're leading a team, it's critical to create the conditions for people to be their best. When you create an environment where people feel open, it triggers their creativity and imagination, it encourages brainstorming and activates the frontal cortex in the brain. This is when people come up with the best ideas and solve major issues you may be challenged with. This does not mean that, as a leader, you must act on every idea/solution your team presents. But it does mean you should let them know that every idea counts. I have always strived to build an environment where people were valued. I believe my optimism and positivity were driving factors in helping people reach their desired goals. Working with me offered them the opportunity to learn new skills and competencies because of the coaching and mentorship they received.

I have read a million leadership books, but never one that articulates exactly how I lead. There are pieces of leadership books that capture different aspects of leadership, and I have learned from many great leaders what to do and what not to do. I have discovered along this journey that sharing and mentoring others is one of the most significant gifts of life.

Leadership can make or break a business, a team, and people. One of the truest statements someone once said to me is this: "If you are not working on the culture, don't think there isn't one. There is always a culture in an organization, store, or district; the problem is it might not be the one you want." So, with or without leadership, there will still be a culture, but will it be the one *you* want? Leaders create good or bad cultures. As a leader who grew up through the ranks of the entire retail food chain from salesperson to vice president, I have seen it all. I have had good bosses and bad bosses, and I've learned that good leadership can only be developed under the right circumstances.

Because of this, I decided it's time to share my leadership concepts with the world. If you take one thing away from this book that helps you be a better leader, a better person, and overall just better in your family and business relationships, then this book will have done its job. Leadership continues to trend high on Google ad words. It's no wonder. Positive leadership that is authentic and genuine pays dividends that last a lifetime. What makes my leadership different from anyone else's? Most likely, like you, I've learned from all the great leaders who have shared their stories through books and talks. I've been told by many who have worked with me that my leadership style allows others to truly be themselves, which today is essential to building a successful business, whatever that may be.

One of my favorite things about working in retail is the people I have worked with. Many of you have helped me towards my path of building a learning and development company that teaches and develops leaders within retail. But as I share my story, I acknowledge it was not an easy nor comfortable journey, and there were people along the way who doubted my ability—including me. I did not follow the traditional route of getting a degree and a higher education in learning. My knowledge comes from life experiences, doing the job and leading large teams, from being a store manager, to a district supervisor, to a regional director, and then to vice president of a national sales and operations team. Back in the day, there was a saying in retail that said, "You do the job, and then you will get the job." I worked hard, made it my mission to work well with others, and strived to add value to those around me.

I haven't always had great experiences as a retail employee. There have been times when I felt my efforts were unappreciated. But today, I am grateful for those times. Without the difficult times, I would not have learned some very important life lessons. Retailu.ca came about because of my desire to teach leaders how to lead and close the gap on retail development programs that just don't work. My goal now is to build retailu into a global brand. I have learned that some situations will challenge you and your confidence. But also, becoming aware of how these moments can propel you toward your dreams, I am grateful and accept every last one of them.

I have also learned that we may not always be aware of the dreams we have. We might only accept the reality we are living in. Your life is a story, and just like a storybook, if you allow it to unfold, you never know where you may land. I started as a retail manager over twenty-five years ago in a city called Manchester. My retail career has taken me to the US, working for Starbucks, Gap Inc., and Apple. It then took me to Canada, where I grew in my career and influence.

Being a single mum, like many in retail, raising two kids alone was not easy, but it wasn't hard either. I had a retail family to help me. Could I have ever seen this coming? Did I ever feel like I chose my career? If I am honest, I didn't. I thought it was by default that I landed in it, like a lot of retail leaders. Moving out of home early, becoming a young mum, and finding a job to provide for myself and my kids, retail became my saving grace. Today, I can see how that long journey and all my experiences helped me find my passion for teaching leaders in retail how to be better leaders. I hope my story and the leadership strategies that have brought me success will provide you with insight that will serve you in your life and business.

Perhaps you are a retail manager like I was. Retail can seem like a thankless job, as is any position in the service industry. At worse, it is often viewed as a job best suited for the young or uneducated. That is why this book is important. These predispositions about retail don't take into account the great life lessons one can gain in their first retail job. Did you know that the retail industry is actually the third-highest employer in the world and generates trillions of dollars for economies worldwide? I bet you didn't know that!

When I moved to Canada in 2006, retail careers were not coveted. These jobs were not viewed as being designed for skilled workers. However, when you think about what a retail manager does, it's kind of mind-boggling. Today, it is recognized, probably because it does take skill to manage a team of people, drive sales of sometimes upwards of a million dollars, and create an environment where customers want to shop. A retail manager's job is diverse and challenging. Some managers manage up to $100 million in sales and lead teams of hundreds of people. But even if you lead a team with just a handful of people, you have the chance to help people develop qualities that can change their lives forever. This is the impact you can have, and it is an amazing opportunity. Creating a positive place for people to work has a significant effect on their wellbeing—just as creating a negative place for people to work does. Sometimes I think they should rename the position "store manager" to "positive change-makers." Because, really, that's what they do!

CHAPTER 1

ACT: Leading with Awareness

AWARENESS IS FAR MORE THAN a buzzword. It is the key to mindful leadership. Mindfulness is a term that is being introduced more and more in business. Meditation has been proven to help us focus and be present. It helps us get into the frontal cortex, which is the creative part of our brains. This is super important for us in today's hyperconnected world. I learned to meditate early on in my thirties. When I moved to Toronto, I needed to find peace from busy days as a single mum and a retail store manager. A friend of mine introduced me to meditation; he said it helped him calm down and release stress. That sounded good to me. I wanted more of that in my life.

Through meditation, I became more self-aware. I started to relax, stay calm, and pay attention to what was happening around me. When other people were stressed and reacting to situations, I was able to disconnect and put myself in the place of an observer. This has helped my leadership dramatically—it has made me happier and more peaceful and allowed me to become an observer with no attachment to the outcome. It has helped me be objective and less judgmental of situations and people.

Learning about Buddhism and meditation taught me that everything is impermanent, like waves in the ocean; no two moments will ever be the same. By letting my ego go, I learned not to take things personally.

The more neutral or removed from the situation I could become, the easier it was to deal with what was happening around me. I didn't know at the time what an influence it had on my leadership, but now I can see that learning how to disconnect and observe my thoughts and emotions helped me become a more self-aware person and a better listener.

Being a twin and watching my sister early on taught me that I could make better choices. When I observed my sister's actions, it was like watching myself on a TV screen; I saw the outcome, but I was removed from it.

For me, leading with awareness means being present, being objective, being neutral, and seeing things for what they are. It's helped me read what is and is not being said in the room and pay attention to the people I interact with in a very intentional way. When you are in a state of awareness, you are fully present. You are not thinking about tonight's dinner or what you will do in the next five minutes. Awareness is about being fully alive at that moment. It is difficult for most of us to practice this kind of awareness, as we are so busy thinking or doing, which I like to call "stuff management." You know, the stuff we manage every day. When we start to practice meditation in our lives, we begin to see things differently. This is what happened to me. I became much more aware of myself.

Taking this level of awareness into leadership is a good thing. When we are present with those we lead, they feel more supported and heard, which in turn helps them feel valued. Studies show that people's top requests from their bosses, friends, and partners are to be heard. Being heard makes them feel supported and accepted. To really hear people, you must be present and fully engaged, which *is* the act of self-awareness. When you are self-aware, you know when you are not present.

Leading with awareness helps me practice a different listening level than I achieve in my regular day. It allows me to get curious because

I am entirely focused on the person in front of me. Being in a state of awareness puts us as leaders in a role where we stop assuming and start asking, we stop judging and start accepting, and we stop telling and start teaching. I used to think meditation meant I had to sit in silence and not think of anything. I have since learned that meditation is not about sitting and thinking of nothing—though it's great if you can. I can't clear my mind of every thought. Meditation is more about being aware of what you are thinking about, because once you are aware of your thoughts, you can change them.

Mindful leadership is about being aware of who we and who our team members are. When we practice mindful leadership, we are suddenly able to pay attention to others by focusing on what is important to them, having an open mind, and really listening to what's being shared and what is spoken in silence. Meditation develops these beneficial human qualities when practiced often. The next meeting you attend or conversation you witness, practice being fully present. Forget about your to-do list, your kid's soccer practice, or where you want to go on vacation this year. Practice being aware of how you show up, how you interact, and how people respond to you. Pay attention to what makes you react, how much you talk, how much others talk, what is shared, and what is unspoken.

Leading with awareness starts with achieving a state of self-leadership and then practicing it with others. Once you commit to self-leadership, you can effectively lead those on your team. When you lead them, you will do so by encompassing three ways of being.

Accept, Create, and Teach

Accept, create, and teach. I can honestly say this was and is my formula for success. As I was climbing the ladder in retail from the salesperson to the vice president of a national retailer, I didn't think about it; I just did it. When I think about what I did, these three behaviors framed the way I led. These are not complicated elements; the *Harvard Business Review on Leadership* does not back them, nor do they have a psychologist's stamp of approval. But they are time-tested and field-proven behaviors that successful leaders demonstrate.

Accepting, creating, and teaching are three human behaviors that have built brilliant, high-performing retail teams, developed businesses, delivered strong results, and won awards during my time as a leader in retail. If that's not enough proof that these three actions work, then I don't know what else is. So, enough suspense. Let's learn what they are!

To lead with awareness, must become aware of what you see and feel and then ACT:

> **Accept**: Be supportive. Avoid judgments and assumptions.

> **Create**: Be responsible. Think and envision possibilities.

> **Teach**: Be selfless. Mentor and coach others.

Let's look at each element in detail.

CHAPTER 2

Accept

To believe or come to recognize (an opinion, explanation, etc.); to be designed; to allow (something to be applied); to take upon oneself, to acknowledge.

Acceptance unites us all.

THE FIRST STEP TO LEADING with awareness is to accept.

This might sound counterintuitive. Why would you accept a situation or person that is not in line with your values and beliefs? Well, read on, and let me tell you why acceptance is so valuable. We all want to be accepted. It's innate. We crave acceptance from our spouses, our families, and our work colleagues. We desire to be accepted by our peers from the time we are toddlers. We look for ways to be recognized or accepted into social groups and work teams, and that desire doesn't go away as we age. It grows over time. While we crave acceptance for ourselves, we sometimes suffer from the propensity to be judgmental toward others. We don't like the way our sister is raising her kids. We dislike the clothes a friend wears. We comment on other people's relationship choices, wondering why they can't see what we can see. We are critical of work colleagues and the projects they complete or the decisions they make. We are good at seeing the flaws of others, but we don't like it when the tables are turned on us. "The No Judgement Zone" is a term coined by Planet Fitness. It was designed to encourage people of all ages and body types to work out in their gyms. They called it "standing up to gym intimidation." They were appealing to that innate need within all of us to be accepted where we are and the desire to feel we belong.

Author Catherine Loving wrote:

> *Judging someone else is the kind of one-way street that always arrives at a dead end. Judging doesn't help us to understand other people, and it can be a sneaky and negative way for us to attempt to feel better about ourselves.*

Is it possible that what we judge as a flaw is a latent talent or strength that might blossom into a great asset for the person and the team with the right coaching and mentorship?

Swedish entrepreneur and author Erik Bolinder rented office space, hired employees, and even provided his top web developer housing. He gave this developer thirty days to complete his software training program. Two weeks into the project, Erik visited the developer. He found that virtually nothing had been done regarding the project, and the developer was sitting on the floor playing video games. But the developer assured Erik that he had been working hard and was making significant progress.

A week later, Erik visited again and found the same scene. No work was completed on the training program, and the developer was sitting on the floor, playing video games. Erik exploded in anger and demanded an explanation of how the developer had been spending his time.

The developer showed Erik a new delivery system that, until this time, had never been done: online training courses. Up to this time, Erik had been delivering his training via VHS tapes and CDs. This new innovation exploded Erik's business, taking him worldwide and increasing sales tenfold. The work the developer needed to complete on the training program only took him three days, and he delivered it ahead of the thirty-day deadline.

People have skill sets they may not be aware of because of their lack of confidence or self-awareness. Others are aware of having those skills and are silently screaming for the opportunity to utilize them. The best managers can identify talent and ability, then build the confidence of those individuals and harness it to benefit both the employee and the company. Even better, great managers give their employees the right culture to thrive and grow so that those abilities bubble to the surface, because these managers are aware of their impact on others' lives. That impact extends far beyond their work life.

I have witnessed people grow and develop themselves into great leaders and shape careers through retail, as well as discover their passion. They have moved on to live their purpose, because the manager they worked for identified and harnessed their unique abilities. This feeling of being accepted and not judged builds people's self-esteem and courage not only in their job but in their personal lives. This is the power of a good boss who creates a positive environment for people.

In retail, our teams constantly judge themselves when sales are low, even though they may have the same team and still do the same things that proved successful in the past. Especially now, with online sales growing, store teams need even more support and acceptance from their leader. It is easier than you think to create a culture where people feel accepted (supporting) rather than judged. Imagine a world where all retail employees feel valued and a sense of belonging.

You only have to go onto Facebook groups of retail workers to know that they do not currently feel prized and appreciated. It breaks my heart when I read negative customer reviews or employees' comments regarding how they feel about the store they work in.

When leaders shared with me that they did not feel supported, it almost always came down to a lack of feeling understood and accepted for their beliefs and values as a human being. The same goes for customers. Think about your relationships and how true this is. Acknowledging and reminding your team how great they are is a powerful tool for fostering your organization's acceptance. After all, each person was hired amid the pool of available candidates because they possessed something the other candidates lacked. That may have been experience, training, knowledge, personality, or just that x-factor that we can never quite seem to put our finger on. Whatever it was, they can utilize those attributes to make the company better with the right leadership.

To be clear, accepting yourself does not imply weakness, giving up, or staying in the same place. Practicing acceptance means respecting the process and acknowledging where you are so you can do something about it. This is easily applied when you lead yourself and others. Practicing the art of acceptance with ourselves first shows vulnerability, and it honors our strengths and weaknesses within our leadership. This helps us to have more compassion. Our self-worth issues usually drive this desire to feel valued. When we start to look at our doubts and insecurities, we can see where our most significant areas of growth reside.

Let me explain.

Acknowledging my own flaws, such as not being highly strategic, is neither good nor bad. It is what it is. It doesn't make me a poor leader. Being self-aware of this flaw makes me a better leader. Why? Because when I acknowledge my own shortcomings, I put a plan in place to ensure that strategic planning is achieved without self-judgment. I know my strengths and weaknesses and mitigate them where needed.

For example, suppose I find someone who is a strategic thinker. I could run my plans by them, or have a strategic meeting expert come in and work with my team, if my deficiency is causing issues. From this perspective and self-awareness, I have learned that this does not make me a poor leader.

Not being strategic and strong at administrative duties has never held me back, because I am not in denial. In fact, I would apologize to my team for this. Being self-aware is critical. If I hadn't been self-aware and did not acknowledge (accept) my deficiencies, it could negatively impact my team. Many leaders are in denial or get defensive when faced with their weaknesses or, even worse, judge themselves and secretly feel that they will be exposed one day for their shortcomings. This can cause significant problems; ego and lack of humility can surface. Either one of these is detrimental to creating a culture where people thrive.

Instead of thinking of situations and people as bad or good, we should just see them for who and what they are. Observe how many times in a day you judge yourself and others. It's pretty eye-opening when you start to practice the art of acceptance in your leadership. You will begin to notice how many times you judge, are biased, and impose that on others. You may also notice how many times you judge your own abilities. I struggled with my self-worth and sense of value for years. So, practicing acceptance has been vital for my growth, which, by the way, is still a work –in progress every day!

To put the A in ACT, these tips can help you:

Accepting Responsibility and Owning Your Part

Taking responsibility and owning what you have done or not done is essential in building trust with others.

We have the opportunity every day to demonstrate this, and when we do, our teams feel supported. This happens a lot, especially when results are not where we want them to be. It is easy to make assumptions about people and why the results are the way they are.

Accepting the harsh reality that your customers may not like your products or policies can be hard to believe. This is because every product bought or policy put in place was done with the best intentions. It's essential to listen to the frontline employees who interact with the customers and live the reality every day on the shop floor. The more I became removed from the sales floor, the bigger the challenge became to hear what the customer was telling me.

A mentor of mine once said that customers vote every day with the money they put in your register. This is so true. This is why I believe in customer insight surveys, which generally validate what your field leaders are already telling you.

If you don't have a "voice-of-the-customer survey" or some other way of completing customer insights, you should put a plan to gather this kind of feedback.

Listening to the customer is crucial. There are many ways you can engage customers to encourage them to provide feedback.

You can set up a customer group page where customers can share feedback or a voice of the customer survey. Live chat is another great tool that gives you direct access to customers and gives them an outlet to praise you or offer their concerns. Monitor your feedback on all major social media outlets by regularly performing a simple search of your company to see what people are saying about your organization.

As you implement strategies for customer feedback, remember your employees are internal customers. As such, you must have methods for receiving their feedback. Their voices are just as important as the customers'. When I was a store manager, I put out anonymous surveys to my team. I remember printing them off and putting them in the break room with a box they could slip them into; I would ask a series of questions on how they felt working in my store and feedback on managers and other initiatives. I did not wait for the company to launch a survey; I wanted to know. My management team appreciated this. It gave us focus and feedback on areas we were exceeding and those needing improvement.

I believe the answers can be found in the field. What I mean by this is if you hold a call with a field leadership team, you better listen to what they say. When I was a vice president, I introduced a communication tool that empowered and engaged the frontline employees to have a voice. It was an app called Nudge, and it allowed me to gather feedback directly, from the part-time person to the full-time manager. I could ask a question and remove all the filters that would have stopped me from getting the raw, honest feedback. I worked to dispel any fear that they would be judged for sharing their honest opinion. This sounds simple, but it is not.

Feeling judged is a real fear in all of us, especially when you need the paycheck at the end of the week. I believe when you set up a culture of nonjudgement and support, your employees will feel safe enough to share what you need to hear, even if you don't want to listen to it!

Here is the kicker: Just like when a customer reviews you on Google, and we listen to them, we should give each employee the same respect and not judge them for *how* they say what they feel, rather we should listen to what they are saying.

Another example of this was when I was head of operations. I invited a group of high-performing store managers to the head office, where we held a workshop to uncover their most significant pain points. We then had the managers present their findings to the heads of departments. This was genius. It helped the departments solve issues they didn't know they had, it engaged the field teams, and it built strong cross-functional relationships, which helped everyone feel supported. It also stopped the negative assumptions between teams and allowed us to face reality and work toward positive solutions together.

Acknowledging and accepting how a team feels about you may mean you have to listen to words that are hard to hear. Every leader needs to face how the team feels about working for them before they can gain buy-in and move forward with the game plan.

Acceptance of how the team feels in any given situation allows the leader to understand and assess progress. Feelings change based on the last conversation you had with someone, so being proactive and aware of this is a key component of leading with awareness.

When I was an assistant store manager at the Banana Republic in Florida, my peers didn't think I was following operational duties with care, because I would miss specific tasks and closing procedures. I felt like this was unnecessary, as I was so great at customer service and engaging with others. I remember my store manager at the time saying to me, "If you want to get promoted and run your own store, your lack of credibility in this area will hinder your peers from respecting you when the time comes." When one gets promoted, she told me that everyone is always looking at what you're not doing, not what you are. So, you better ensure you get the simple things right. Other challenges will warrant more acceptance from your team versus not completing a safe log on a closing shift. This was a huge lesson learned. I then checked my work three times to ensure I didn't give them reasons to pull it apart. I got promoted, and everyone supported me on the team.

To ensure you are demonstrating this, do the following:

- Ask for feedback constantly by using open-ended questions.
- Have your team complete surveys to provide anonymous feedback.
- Practice asking your customers who are shopping for feedback.
- Step back and ensure your personal biases are not getting in your way.
- Observe and become detached from the outcome.
- Help others feel their opinions matter by listening and not interrupting or justifying.
- Practice engaged listening, put everything in your head aside, and show that you care by making the person you engage with your top priority.

Accepting Feedback and Asking Questions

It is important to accept what others are telling you, but just as important is to act on what is being shared if it is negatively impacting others and your business. I have received many examples of constructive feedback, even though it's tough to accept, I always try to see it as a gift and assume positive intent when it's being delivered.

An example of this was when I worked within a team of leaders that felt I was too competitive and did not listen. This happened twice in my career—the first time I accepted it and made the necessary changes. In the second situation, I accepted that the organization just wasn't for me. Either way, it was essential to listen and ask questions of the leaders providing it, along with questioning myself. At the end of the day, if someone feels a certain way about my leadership, it is their reality, even if it's not mine, and it is my job to change that perception.

When I was an assistant manager, I remember receiving a complaint about my communication from someone on the team. He felt that I always picked on him and gave him more work when closing the store. I was not aware of this at all. It shocked me when I heard this, and my first reaction was to defend myself and judge him and his performance. But when I paused and reflected on his feedback, I felt terrible he felt this way. So instead of judging him and defending myself, I decided to change how I talked to him and tailored my approach to help him feel encouraged, not discouraged. We have all received feedback that we felt was not warranted, but what's important is that we react to it in a way that creates a safe space for our teams to be open, feel supported and continue to share when things are not going well for them.

I find it helpful when receiving feedback to reflect on it for twenty-four hours. It's tough to get feedback that requires you to change and improve, especially when you don't think you need to; we all need to grow continually, and most times, when we are given feedback from others, there is always some truth in it, even if it's just the way the other person feels. Accepting how others feel and focusing on them versus focusing on yourself is very difficult for most leaders. *Why?* Because of ego. Our egos want to protect us and tell us that we are right. One thing I always told my ex-husband was, "You can win the argument, but you won't win my heart!" This is an incredibly true statement when you apply it in the work setting.

Being a true leader is about showing humility. If being right is more important than understanding how someone else feels, good luck building a team!

Accept Your Strengths and Opportunities, Embrace the Same in Your Team

One of the worst things I have witnessed leaders do is blame their people when things are not going right. Looking in the mirror and accepting our shortcomings and how these affect your team will help you teach them to do the same. One of my biggest flaws is that I am not strategic. At times, I don't think long-term, and I am risk-averse.

One of my strengths is staying positive while managing ambiguity and taking each day at a time. This can frustrate a team that needs structure and long-term vision; instead of changing this, I accept it openly, and I discuss and share it with those around me. Now, as an entrepreneur, it serves me well, and my business partner Jane is the one who is a detailed planner and keeps me grounded.

Accepting your areas of expertise and improvement will allow you to show a vulnerable side. Be careful to remember what I shared in the beginning.

When sharing your vulnerable side, it is still essential to lead your team well. A team wants a competent leader who is knowledgeable and can teach them something. Before making a plan, be realistic about what you and your team can achieve. Having realistic expectations is so important. If you expect them to work miracles without providing them with the resources to achieve the goals, your expectations are not realistic, and your team will feel defeated.

Whenever I hear managers say they feel unsupported by their leader or the company, it usually stems from not feeling heard, which translates into feeling judged and not accepted by their leader.

A few of my favorite questions to ask managers when I visited stores were:

- What helps you feel supported?
- What makes you feel least supported?
- How can we support you achieve what we are asking of you?
- What does support mean to you?

There are many different answers, but in my experience, it all stems from the leader they work for. Ultimately, at a store level, it is their district manager. At a district manager level, it becomes more about the company strategy and resources. It is far more apparent at a director level that it's about budgets, company direction, and tools to execute. We need to truly understand this to move forward to the next step in Leading with Awareness, which is to *Create*. Without the first step of *Accept* in action, creating becomes much more challenging.

Face Reality

Acknowledge the current situation, and face reality for what it is. Accepting the current reality is very difficult for most leaders, as it requires complete neutrality—no assumptions—and only fact-finding. It calls you to acknowledge the moment for what it is. It is neither good nor bad. It involves forming no opinion on what is occurring and placing no particular investment on the outcome.

I once worked with a manager in Florida who would say, "It is what it is."

Why is this so difficult? Because leaders think they know best. They shape the narrative of their feelings, perspectives, and experiences. They determine the most factual reality through their own lenses, based on their own biases and assumptions. This is quite normal for all of us. We are emotional human beings and, given a title, can become caught up in the lure of the management hierarchy. We think that having a title means we should know the answers. If you are like me, you want to jump into action and get things moving fast.

I have learned, every team and business is different. Your view is based on how you feel, what you have observed, and your past experiences. You must understand there is another layer of reality. The reality of how your team feels in any given situation. Yes, how they feel. This is a crucial factor.

One of the worst things any leader can do is assume they know the answers and fail to ask members of the team their opinions or, even worse, ask them but not accept what they are saying.

Accepting the current circumstances means you have to face the reality of what your team is telling you. If you ignore the reality of what your people are telling you, it will demotivate and disengage your team in the quest for solutions. Hearing things you don't want to hear is also very difficult for leaders. However, sometimes people will tell you what you need to hear versus what you want to hear. But this can only happen if you help them feel like they are in a safe space to open up and share.

As a senior leader, I acknowledged that my title preceded me—I tell leaders this when I coach them. Being aware of this is crucial for seeing reality and creating an environment where people can be sincere and open. I had to work hard when I was a vice president to make people feel I was not automatically smarter and better than them just because of my title. I wanted to ensure that when I visited stores, they felt so comfortable I could hear their reality with no judgment to understand the real pain points of our customers and employees.

This was especially important to me because when I was a store manager, I remember holding those dreaded head office visits where everything had to be perfect for the visitors.

My district manager at the time would ask us to over-schedule hours, stay late, and make the store picture-perfect so that the visit would go well. The one problem I always had with this was how my head office partners could support me and help solve issues if they don't see the real picture. I remember when the vice president of stores said to me at the time, "Wow, your tables look so perfect, and that khaki wall, how do you keep it this way?"

In my head, I was dying to say that we don't, but the look on my district manager's face staring right at me was intense. My answer was that it's a challenge. I vowed if I ever got to a vice president role, I would never set this unrealistic expectation for me and my title, and I would set the expectation that our stores should be visit-ready for our customers every day.

If you are a senior leader and hold a title, accept this is something needing your attention. Acknowledging and accepting this as part of your reality is a must. You can then think about what you can do to disarm people from judging you by your title and make them feel safe.

One thing I used to say is, "Hi, I am April, a person just like you, and vice president is just my job title." This would make people feel at ease. Can you think of anyone you have ever worked with who does this well? What do they do? How did it make you feel? Did you want to work harder? And *why*?

Acceptance is the opposite of resistance, which is key to living a happy, healthy, harmonious life and one that will bring more of what you want to you. The laws of cause and effect tell us what we focus on more will come to be; when we resist the reality of what we are facing, what we resist persists.

To move on to the next step in leading with awareness, we need to face reality and acknowledge where we are. Without this, creating and envisioning will be a challenge. When I moved to Canada as a mum with two kids, I had to accept this reality and build my life to work around being a single parent and a retail manager. It was challenging to face this reality. I struggled with my desire to move up in my career while balancing my responsibilities. Sometimes we need to accept where we are to move forward. One of my favorite bosses used to say to me, "Hope is not a plan." She was right.

Start with Self

Approach setbacks in a positive way. A positive mind and not being hard on yourself are essential when you lead others. When you acknowledge you are capable of doing better, any shortcomings seem to matter less. This has a dramatic effect on the morale of your team. It may take effort, but there is always something good—even in bad situations. The ability to move forward positively means you can accept yourself and the situation for what it is entirely.

We all want acceptance, and we know how important it is to accept the things we cannot change. Research shows: our willingness to accept the unchangeable has a great deal to do with our emotional and psychological well-being. I'll bet your experiences have taught you that as well. Fighting or resisting what you cannot change will cause more resistance and stress in your life. What most people think is that acceptance means we forget; the truth is quite the opposite. It doesn't minimize the significance of what happened; it just means being willing to acknowledge what is without resisting or denying it.

In recapping *Accept,* we can put it into five steps:

1. **Face reality**
2. **Nix judgement—see the good**
3. **Approach setbacks in a positive way**
4. **Check your biases—stay neutral**
5. **Stay present—manage the moment**

Start with yourself, and then practice this with others.

CHAPTER 3

Create

Create /kre-'ate:

cause (something) to happen as a result of one's actions.

WHEN WE THINK OF THE word *create*, it evokes images of artists, designers, and marketing teams who manage creative teams, or simply being a creative person who builds concepts and ideas and imagines new possibilities.

When you are leading with *awareness,* create means to be responsible with your thoughts, words, actions, and behaviors. My all-time favorite book, *The Science of Mind*, by Ernest Holmes, tells us that what we think about comes into reality, due to the universal law of cause and effect. Let me share an example of how this law works.

My passion for developing others has sparked my love for working in retail. So, when I saw a job posted for a director of learning and development, I naturally believed that the universe was giving me a sign. I loved my job and worked for one of the best bosses in my career—a great leader who was a teacher. We had an excellent team, and it felt so good to be part of a start-up in retail. I felt like I had hit the jackpot. I learned a lot, met amazing people, and created strong relationships that I still enjoy today.

However, the retail landscape was changing. A new president came on board. He decided to change the brand's direction, closed the division, and moved my awesome boss to a new position in the organization, leaving many of us devastated and thinking about what we should do next. As I said, I thought the universe was giving me a sign that maybe I should move into a learning and development role, so I went to the HR director to apply.

I was super excited about the meeting and thought this could be the perfect opportunity to transition from an operations role to helping the organization develop its leaders; it sounded so perfect. I will never forget this conversation; I still remember it like it was yesterday. There have been many events in my life that, at the time, might have felt harsh—upon reflection, they were pivotal moments that propelled me forward. At this time, I had just started to envision what retailu could look like and was thinking about how this role could teach me a lot, along with what I could bring from an operations perspective to the learning and development team.

When I reached her office, she proceeded to say, "This won't take long." She asked me why I was interested in the role. I shared my passion for learning, development, and teaching others. She then proceeded to tell me how my goals were great, but because I had no formal education in learning and development or human resources, I was not qualified for the job. She noted that I didn't know how to format a learning program, which at the time was true. She told me I would never get a job in learning and development because of this; of course, I was disappointed.

For the next thirty days, I searched online for courses I could take to start educating myself. One afternoon, I was surfing Facebook, and the John C. Maxwell coaching program popped up. I emailed them, and one year later I became a certified coach. One year after that, I started retailu as a blog, and one year after that, I incorporated retailu as an online e-learning site. I could have been mad at my HR direector for not giving me a chance or even could have taken her advice and stayed in my comfort zone. However, I now own a learning and development company, and I am forever grateful to her for that conversation, as it was the spark that activated me to build something I felt could add value to retailers.

When you have setbacks, positively approaching them and focusing your mind on what you want will help you manifest them in reality. This is the true reflection of creating what you want. Sometimes it's hard for us and our teams to see what's possible, because it may be so far away from our reality.

For example, building an online learning platform was not something I could have imagined six years ago. I knew I wanted to continue to develop others in a more meaningful way. I spent my time and efforts growing my leadership skills and learning to follow that passion, even though I didn't have a formal education. It was what I always wanted to do. The *how* just seemed to happen along the way through a series of random people who taught me how to build retailu.

The main point here is that I was passionate and took responsibility for my thoughts and then acted on them. The universe guided me along the path by introducing mentors over the past five years who educated me on how to build an e-learning platform and make videos, and who helped me get what was in my head into the courses.

This is why I believe it is crucial for us to be responsible for our attitude, thoughts, and focuses. If I hadn't used my experience to test this theory, I could have missed the opportunity to help retailers and train thousands of leaders globally. Because my desire was so strong, and because I spent my time actively taking actions that would get me closer, the universe brought the right people into my life at the right time, and retailu was born.

Sometimes it's hard to see the path to achieve our dreams. If you spend time thinking more about what you want and are willing to learn from others, the law of cause and effect will eventually catch up to you. Here's how it happened to me:

Through a Facebook ad, I met a lady who lived in Costa Rica who had an online business. She introduced me to a man who lived in Toronto, a guru in online marketing and selling courses. He told me six years ago, when I was ready to make my courses, to reach out to him; at the time, I thought he was crazy! Me, write courses and build an e-learning site? I was a director of sales who wanted to build teams and develop leaders. Then, while attending a mentorship call, the John C. Maxwell team president said one thing to me that changed the trajectory of my coaching and leadership journey.

One Saturday afternoon, I was openly sharing on a training call on how hard it was to gather a bunch of random people and start a mastermind. Part of becoming a certified Maxwell coach was to host a mastermind; this is where you bring a group of people together and discuss John's books weekly. I was trying to build my coaching and mastermind business to exit retail after almost two decades training leaders to be better leaders with his content. I will never forget this comment, as it turned the light switch on that helped me envision what retailu could become. He said, "April, why are you trying to leave retail? Why aren't you making retail work for you?" He was right. Why didn't I take all my years of experience and what I had learned through the Maxwell program, along with my knowledge, and create something unique? Paul mentored me back on his weekly calls; he would focus on mindset and my thoughts. I remember his favorite thing to say was, "Hold your vision." My vision was to develop leaders. At the time, I didn't exactly know how that was going to translate this into reality; six years later, here we are.

I have always taught my kids the philosophy of envisioning. I believe that if you think and envision whatever you want, it will eventually come about, as long as you are willing to put in the effort to get there. A year ago, my son and I were having dinner, and he asked if I believed talent superseded work ethics. "Good question," I answered. "Well, I believe that if you find your talent and add work ethics to it, you will be more successful than demonstrating one or the other."

I also shared with him that you must first think about what you want and then write it down to make it a reality. I truly believe in positive affirmations and sending them out into the universe. This creates the energy that will move your desires into your reality. This is why strategic planning is essential, because when your team is aligned, you have a much better chance of achieving your goals.

Because of this conversation, a year ago my son wrote down his affirmations. I love my kids, because they are always willing to try something new. So, he wrote them down, and we put them in a place where they would be undisturbed. A year later, I sent him a picture of it, and guess what? At sixteen, he has created exactly what he visualized a year ago—playing basketball on a full scholarship in a high school in Florida. There are a few items on the list that have not yet come to reality. Nevertheless, I am sure that I will see them manifest in his life within the following year.

To help you understand the power of this quality, let me tell you a story about when I became more aware of how powerful this is in the business environment. I was working as a director for a fashion retailer, and we received news that a new VP was starting and would be my boss. I was excited but also nervous. My anxiety was further heightened by the fact that we were in the middle of Black-Friday planning.

Our goals were increased from last year's sales, and I was laser-focused on what we had to achieve and execute at the store level to achieve such large sales targets. Not that sales targets are stressful, but a lot goes on behind the scenes for this one-day event, as you know if you work in retail. Black Friday is an event that has become an entire week of promotions, emails, merchandise changes, and scheduling to meet the workload demands and provide excellent customer service—all while keeping everyone happy and motivated to deliver.

I remember this day so clearly. It was a Wednesday afternoon, and we had scheduled a meeting with the different departments to plan out our strategy and figure out what we were going to do to drive sales and win the holiday season. Our new VP came into the session in the middle of the meeting, which we were not expecting. We were all excited to meet her; she asked us what we were working on, so we went through and shared the plan. I will never forget this moment, as it was one of the best leadership lessons in my career. After presenting the plan and sales goal, she turned to us all and said the sales are not good enough; you will need to increase it and deliver X amount more to hit X target.

Really? What did she know? She had just walked into the business and had no history or idea of our traffic or what was possible in sales. She then exited the room. We all sat there deflated and then spent the next forty-five minutes discussing who would get up the nerve to go and tell her that her request was ridiculous, absurd, and impossible. We had never hit the number she mentioned and never generated enough traffic to come close. Instead of strategizing about sales, we got sidetracked talking about whether to tell her. Guess who got nominated? Of course, I was!

Later that afternoon, I went down to her office and asked for a moment of her time. I explained and told her why the number she had provided was not possible and presented all the reasons why. She looked at me and said, "April, if you don't believe it, you won't achieve it."

She then turned to her computer, went back to typing, and I exited the office. Needless to say, that plan didn't go as I had hoped. I went home that night and thought about how I would tell the rest of the team.

Accepting where you are is sometimes challenging. But these were the circumstances: I had been given a new boss who had no idea in my book, so what was I going to do? I went home, drove to the dollar store, bought a bunch of large gold-wrapped chocolate bars, and then proceeded to design a one million dollar bill on my mac, which was the sales goal we were expected to hit. I added the company logo, wrapped the chocolate bars in this branded one million dollar bill, and went to bed.

The next day I went to the office early and placed one on every person's desk. I mailed them to the stores and made sure every manager on the team had one. I then sent out an email and said, when we hit the one million goal, we would celebrate and eat these one million dollar chocolate bars. Those chocolate bars stared at us every day. And we stared back at them. We never again spoke of how we could not meet the goal. Instead, we went to work, figuring out how to hit it. And guess what? We passed the one million dollar sales goal by one hundred thousands dollars. It was another huge lesson learned. Thinking and envisioning what you can't see is hard, but when you lead others, it's a must. Sometimes, we need to create a picture for those around us, take responsibility, and move everyone, including ourselves, towards the unknown.

If you have never practiced the activity of building a vision board, then maybe you should. It is a powerful exercise that can be done in your personal and professional life. This is a daily routine practice in my life. Four years ago, I was on a trip to New York with friends. We had booked a hotel in Times Square. We were on our way out one night, and I saw an easel in the lobby with an itinerary on it with bus pickups and times of a conference. I didn't know what conference it was, but I noticed that it was a retail conference. I thought to myself that this was probably something I should attend and was curious as to why I didn't know about it. However, due to my busy plans for the weekend with my friends, I thought no more about it and went to dinner.

Every time I walked past the easel over the next couple of days, it kept getting stuck in my head to research it and plan to attend next time. I left New York, went home, and carried on as usual. Fast forward a couple of years, and my team asked if we could attend a retail conference in New York. I said, "Of course." During the planning to attend this conference, I was asked if I would participate as a speaker. Since we were already going, I agreed.

I will never forget the day we arrived in New York. My ops manager said we should meet at the hotel, and we would plan our day from there. Great! I loved spending time with my team. I walked into the hotel not knowing, since I hadn't booked it, that it was the same hotel I had stayed in four years earlier. The conference I wanted to attend back then had the same conference sponsor, and now I was a featured panelist. This is why I believe that what you think about really does come about.

These are just a few examples, but it is clear to me in life that the law of cause and effect is very real. As a leader, I have a responsibility to ensure that my mind is clear to create and not get bogged down with "stuff management." This is what being responsible means to me. It means not only taking responsibility physically but mentally, too.

When you think and envision for your business, major shifts can happen. This demonstrates mindful leadership in the best way possible. I also believe we create the conditions for our teams to thrive when we do this. A great activity to complete with your team is to build a vision board of words that exemplify the culture, values, and behaviors you would like to see demonstrated in your organization.

To start to become more of a creator, you will need to change your language.

Remove from your language	Add into your language
I can't.	I can.
I don't know how.	I will learn how.
I am scared.	I am excited.
I am not sure.	I am resourceful.
I will never be able to.	I am able to.

As a leader of any organization, your ability to put your thoughts and efforts in the right direction every day will direct your team into the right actions. But, to be able to do this, you must take time to think. One of the most significant barriers for leaders to overcome and to demonstrate, in action, is to stop spending time thinking with concern, worry, and fear. Another is to take the time to think, period. In today's busy reactionary and unstable retail environment, this in itself is a challenge for most of us.

If we have the power to "think into results," as Bob Proctor—a guru of our times in teaching mindset—would have us believe, we must be responsible for our time, energy, and what we spend our time thinking about. I had the opportunity to take my business partner to one of Proctor's talks in Toronto recently. It was a small, intimate group. Jane had never attended or read anything like this before. I knew it was going to be vital for us to get our thinking on the same page to grow retailu, because I believe in the power of this so much. Since

Jane attended this event, she has been more aware, and together we are constantly thinking about keeping the business healthy and growing.

Just like being positive and smiling more influences our teams, so does what we think. A leader who previously worked for me called me recently and said she was not happy in her current role. As she continued to share what she was going through, it was evident it had started to affect her home life. Simply put, it was stressing her out. My advice was to stop focusing on what was wrong and instead write out what she wanted in her perfect job. I asked her to think about it, document it, and call me back the next day.

She did what I asked of her. I then suggested she put it on a wall somewhere she could see it and read it out loud daily and focus her thoughts on the perfect job. A couple of weeks later, I received a call from her telling me she had received an invitation to attend an interview with one of her dream organizations, and two weeks later, she received a job offer.

Under normal circumstances, we would have most likely jumped into action-planning and missed the most important step: to envision and think. Why do we do this? Because we are so focused on results and the outcome, we spend our time there instead of thinking and getting our minds right. This is hard to teach in business, because it can be perceived as a spiritual idea; however, all the greats such as Wayne Dyer and others have introduced this concept. I believe the leaders who understand this concept and apply it in their business will have far better results. I know this because I have witnessed it repeatedly in my personal and business life.

The challenge for leaders is to accept reality, take responsibility, own their thinking, and move into a mental discipline of not focusing on what we don't want but focus on what we do. Therein lies the challenge. This fundamental coaching on mindset and thinking is not yet something that is embraced in the business world.

When I reflect on my success in business, it is because my life values have translated into how I lead others. I would spend time on a Monday thinking about what it was I wanted to achieve with my store visits, conversations, and meetings for the week. I believe in the future: leaders' thoughts can determine the success of their performance and the performance of others, and they should take time to think intentionally.

Have you ever engaged in the practice of envisioning and thinking intentionally about your business?

What I mean by this is to envision what's possible, which can be a group activity and not too hard to do if you approach it as a goals/visioning strategy session. The next step would be to sit with your vision in your mind intentionally every day for thirty days and see what comes to fruition. I spend time on my insight's timer app every day to get my thinking right. Thinking positively is essential for us to create a place that attracts talent and results.

"*Create!*" This is something I have practiced for years. I am not saying I don't have fearful thoughts, but now as an entrepreneur I am even more aware of taking responsibility for my thinking and how it affects those around me.

In recapping *Create*, it is essential to know that decisions happen here. Envision the future you want to manifest, and take responsibility for your thinking before anything else.

It can be thought about in the following five steps:

1. **Be responsible for what you think.**
2. **Be accountable for how you spend your time.**
3. **Envision the bigger picture.**
4. **Be open. Be positive, and let go of ego.**
5. **Be mindful of others and how they fit into the picture.**

CHAPTER 4

Teach

*To teach is to mentor and coach. This is pretty
straightforward; teaching and mentoring
require commitment and effort.*

"Mentoring is a brain to pick, an ear to listen, and
a push in the right direction."—John Crosby

*We're here for a reason. I believe a bit of the
reason is to throw little torches out to lead people
through the dark.*—Whoopi Goldberg
*Tell me, and I forget; teach me, and I may remember;
involve me, and I learn.* —Benjamin Franklin

*A mentor is someone who allows you to see the
hope inside yourself.*—Oprah Winfrey

I GENUINELY BELIEVE PEOPLE WHO work in retail are a powerful positive force in the world. Nearly every person in the world encounters someone in a retail capacity every week. When you think about this and the power one act of kindness can have on another, I would argue that when you work in retail, you can shape the future behaviors of others more than you realize.

So, what is the best way to affect this powerful and amazing change? Teaching! Retail managers have the unique opportunity to mentor dozens, if not hundreds, of people throughout their careers. They can coach people on how to work effectively in the business space, for sure.

But there is so much more that employees can learn from their retail manager. One of the most rewarding things to do as a retail field leader is to develop others and help them grow. I know this after touring hundreds of retail stores and meeting many retail managers, from the store manager level to the director.

Whenever I ask them what the favorite part of their job is, the number one answer I hear is that they love to coach, train, and develop others. There is nothing more rewarding for them than when they help another person grow, whether in their personal growth or career.

Retail operations teams teach life skills to others; they teach people skills. Working in retail for so long, I have met many leaders. The best leaders I have worked with are those who have a passion for people, keep it simple, and teach and mentor their teams.

As John C. Maxwell wrote in the book *Developing the Leader Around You*, reproducing producers is the highest calling of every leader. The measure of a successful leader is one who can walk away, go on vacation, and their team functions without them.

When I visit stores and districts and hear leaders tell me they never get a day off because their team always calls them, my alarm bells start to ring. They are proud of sharing how they support their team by providing the answers—even when they are supposed to be away for work. I challenge them on this. This is not something to be proud of. In my book, it means that you have not developed your leaders.

I learned this early on in my career. I would get calls from my team when I was a store manager, and I realized that it was because I hadn't taught them what to do, and they felt I didn't trust them. This was a hindrance. Letting go of control and allowing my team to take ownership and learn was hard, but a lesson I needed to learn to help my team grow, which ultimately helped me grow.

Retail operators are in the trenches coaching and leading teams and teaching people how to be better and act selflessly. However, letting go and developing others to take ownership of the business and make their own decisions can be challenging. Why? Because we think we know best, or we just don't know how to develop others. Directing our teams and telling them what to do will not help them in the long run. We can also get frustrated and lack patience with people; what seems common sense to us may not be to someone else. It is essential to see your role as a teacher, as it will make you less frustrated and more present, mindful, and patient with others. This means that even when you work with people who are not in your field of expertise, you approach them with a teaching and mentorship attitude.

A good example of this was in my last job, where I worked cross-functionally with different departments. I could be frustrated and ask myself, *Why don't they understand what happens in a store?* Or I could change the approach to assume positive intent and educate them on our area of the business. My job was to help them help us. I will share more about this later in the book.

Having this approach is helpful, and being helpful stems from being kind. Kindness is a human quality that is necessary to have in a leadership role. There is no room for leaders who do not have this quality. We have a new generation coming into the workforce, and their biggest expectation is to be mentored and provided with the skills to perform and grow in their job. I remember a lesson I learned early on in my retail career from a director, a lesson I carried throughout my entire career. It was honestly the best advice I ever received when I was a store manager at Banana Republic.

I was nominated to participate with a group of managers at a roundtable with a senior director team. I was so excited, and I remember driving to Boca to the head office with a group of my peers, talking about what we were going to ask them. At the time, I was an acting store manager;

I had no idea my retail career would take me to run retail operations for a national chain in Canada. I didn't even know if retail was something I wanted to stay in until a director shared his journey with us. The funny thing about learning from others is sometimes they don't always know the impact of what they say. That day in Boca, a regional director shared a lesson that impacted my leadership and those around me. I remember sitting at a lovely round table; two men entered the room. One was the regional director, and the other was his boss. Each of my peers had the opportunity to ask their questions and learn from these two gentlemen, provide feedback, etc. When it was my turn, I candidly said to him, "What's the best advice you can give to me as a young manager who wants to be in your shoes one day?"

Everyone else had focused on product feedback or operational challenges, but I asked a leadership question. Don't ask me why that came out. I have no idea, and after I said it, I was nervous as the room went silent. Not knowing what he was going to say, I waited nervously for his answer. He proceeded to share his story. He said that when he had joined the company as an assistant manager and was working for a store manager who always told him he would never get anywhere in retail because he was too nice. She said he needed to be tougher and should stop being so friendly with the rest of the team if he ever wanted to get promoted.

Thankfully, he said he was so happy and such a positive person he never took her advice! Not long after that conversation, she was fired for poor behavior, and he was promoted to store manager. Long story short, he developed through the organization into a district manager and then a regional manager. He asked us this simple question: "When you go home at night, what do you spend your time talking about at the dinner table?" We all shared comments typically on how our day went, funny stories from customers and staff, and the interactions with our boss, good or bad, but mostly when they were negative.

"Precisely!" He said and continued to tell us that a manager can make them have a good or a bad day when leading a team. He learned that no matter what, this philosophy had never served him wrong, as a nice person who treats people well. His manager was fired, and he got promoted. He proceeded to say, "Don't let anyone tell you that being too nice will never get you anywhere. Just like we want our team to be nice to our customers, we want our team to love coming to work, and we need to show niceness to them. All of this comes down to one major factor: how they feel about working for you."

He went on to challenge us by saying, "The next time you are working in your store before the end of the day, I want you to reflect on how you spoke to your people and what they would say about you at the dinner table with their loved ones." He told us to think about the ripple effect we wanted to create and how this affects the store and our customers. Powerful! This stuck with me, and no matter what, I have strived to ensure that everyone on my team goes home excited to come back the next day! People may be having a tough day or week, but going to work and being part of a positive, winning team can lift you, inspire you and make a bad day the best you've ever had.

The alternative is to have those loved ones at home telling your employees to leave your team and find another one where they are appreciated and respected. The regional director didn't know it at the time, but this conversation in the room with a group of managers was a development conversation that changed the way I lead for the rest of my entire retail career. These kinds of conversations and teaching moments are invaluable to team members. Everyone at the table that day was focused on operations and products, which was important. I was focused on growth and how to develop my skills. If I had not asked this question, we might not have learned this valuable lesson. Most people want growth. It is a powerful retention tool. People love to be challenged and to learn. I am addicted to learning about leadership. I do this so I can pass on my knowledge to others. I have learned that reading has given me the capacity to learn and open my mind, along with the language to share concepts with those I lead.

One of the best things you can ask your team during or after a store visit or touch base is, "What did you learn today?" I use this question as a pulse check to validate if I was teaching and developing my team. If they couldn't answer, I would follow up with, "What would you like to learn today?" and then we refocus on learning and development. Retention is a big problem in retail, and leaders who teach and mentor, motivate their employees to stay working for them longer than those that don't. Telling and directing are not teaching and mentoring, even though they can seem very similar.

Along with teaching and mentorship, words and body language matter; energy is contagious. And yours, as a leader, will have a direct influence on the way your team feels about what they do. Never take this for granted. Always assume positive intent; this creates a proactive approach to managing people. This does not mean you shouldn't be honest and share feedback with people that can help them improve. Accountability is development; be mindful of what you say and how you say it, and how you present yourself—words matter. The story I shared earlier was a great mentorship conversation that impacted how I led for the rest of my career. It was a story that had so many lessons in it. How to stay confident in who you are, how being a kind leader matters, and the impact of leadership on others. These kinds of moments are invaluable to a leader and can't be learned in a textbook. Think about this the next time you interact with someone on your team. What do you think they learned from you that would impact how they feel working for you, and how would someone feel working for them? This is the power of mentorship.

I worked at Apple for just under a year. One workshop I attended was about mentorship. They asked us to write a letter to someone we admired and would consider a mentor. We were to thank them in the letter and let them know what we had learned from them and explain why we appreciated their mentorship. I will never forget this exercise; it had a lasting impression on me. I wrote a letter to my previous district manager, Mary Downing, who I had worked for at Starbucks in Florida. I thanked her for the attributes I appreciated about her leadership and why I saw her as a mentor.

Once we had completed this exercise, we were asked to reflect on whether someone would write a letter about us in this way. It made me stop and think. I was not sure if someone would write a letter thanking me for being their mentor. I had worked with many leaders to this point, but I could not say if they saw me as a mentor and if I was even thinking about myself as a leader in this way. From that day on, I made it my mission to be a mentor and teach others what was valuable to them, in their opinion, and what I believed would help them grow. I think this is why I still receive emails, Facebook messages, and phone calls from people asking for advice. If someone emails me through LinkedIn and asks me if I would be willing to have a mentorship call with them, I say yes whenever possible. I remember a young student emailing me through LinkedIn while I was a director at Holt Renfrew. She asked me if she could come and work for me.

To graduate, she had to work a total of sixty hours and gain Canadian work experience. When I met her, I quickly realized that she had a ton of retail experience from her past life before she moved to Canada from India. I was happy to have her help, and she assisted me in building the operational procedures and was a tremendous support. She shared that she had emailed five directors, and I was the only one who had responded. I left the organization; that young girl went on to be promoted, worked in the buying team, then moved to New York and joined a massive brand as an assistant buyer, and her career took off. Why am I sharing this story? Because she told me that five other directors did not respond to her initial email, yet once she had joined my team and they met her, everyone wanted her on their team. They assumed that, as a student, she was going to need lots of attention and training. They thought it wasn't worth the time and effort for only sixty hours; however, she became a top employee who has done amazing things. I now have a friend in New York climbing the retail ladder. I always respond to people; I believe this is called human kindness. We all need to think about this, especially if we have the experience that can help mentor and coach others. I mentored her, but she gave me so much in return.

This is why I write a blog and post on LinkedIn to share life lessons and hopefully pass on knowledge and information that can help others. I love to teach and coach others.

One person I admire is my best friend, whom I have known for over two decades. Since both of us have been in retail forever, we have the best conversations and always learn from each other. These are the best kinds of relationships. Being a mentor and coach is knowing what you don't know, seeking advice, and being willing to reach out to others. I have done this my entire career.

This is why *Teach* is the last pillar in leading with awareness.

As I have said, leading with awareness is not a complicated model; it's not study-proven to change behaviors. It didn't result from a survey that I have completed. These three pillars are how I lead. If you asked previous team members, I think they would say they always felt supported and encouraged to be themselves.

Because of step one, they were open to steps two and three.

Teach can be recapped in the following five steps.

1. **Be a student of life.**
2. **Be intentional about developing skills that can help others.**

3. **Be open to hear others' views and experiences.**
4. **Give back to your team through mentorship.**
5. **Be the teacher—not the manager.**

In summary, to ACT—to accept, create, and teach—is a way of being; it is the path to leading as an enlightened leader. Becoming aware of who you are and what you buy into is more than just reading this book. It is a way of being in every moment of every day. The road to a positive life is to remember that what you give is what you get. The laws of the universe are exact. If you want to be happy and successful, remember these three pillars. To lead others is one of the highest callings in life, in my opinion.

It is a huge responsibility: treat it as such.

CHAPTER 5

Finding Purpose

A Life Lesson

You can ask people what *they do for a living. Or you can ask them if they* love *what they do for a living. Everyone's purpose is different and unique to them. Ask yourself these questions, and see what comes up.*

THE SEARCH FOR PURPOSE IS as old as humanity. Scientists confirm that people who function daily from a place of purpose are happier, healthier, and contribute more to the world around them. Without purpose, humanity would never have been able to make the great strides it has made over millennia. It has been key to our ability to adapt, survive, and thrive. We are innately driven by that sense of striving toward a goal. In a CNBC article, leadership researcher Zameena Mejia reports:

> A new study by a team of the Harvard School of Public Health researchers finds that if you feel you have a higher sense of purpose in life — defined as having meaning, a sense of direction, and goals, you are more likely to remain healthy and physically strong as you grow older, ... the study published in the medical journal *JAMA Psychiatry,* the Harvard researchers asked, "Is a higher purpose in life associated with a lower likelihood of declines in physical function?" ... To test if having purpose truly does help you live a longer, healthier life, researchers collected data twice—once in 2006

and again in 2010—from the Health and Retirement Study, an ongoing nationally representative study of American adults over 50 ...

Other studies by the lead researcher Eric Kim have found that a higher sense of purpose also correlates to a reduced risk of disability, stroke, heart disease, sleep issues, and other health problems ... The Harvard researchers noted that, since your sense of purpose can evolve or grow, making sure that you develop yours can improve "not only mental health but physical function as well."

But how is purpose formed? And once it is formed, how do we identify and operate within it? A common misconception about finding purpose is that it springs directly from our inherent gifts and talents. That is true to a point, but it falls far short of encapsulating the essence of purpose. If you are open to others around you, they may help you find your purpose through shared experiences without you even knowing it. Being connected to the right people can help shape your ultimate destiny. As you think about how to ACT with your teams, it would be helpful to do so with a clear sense of purpose. Finding my purpose has been a long journey for me. Having self-worth issues, I didn't always allow myself to believe that my life had a more significant meaning. I also took for granted what I thought was easy, so easy that it must not be worth anything.

If you are struggling with this, think about what makes you happy and what brings you joy, as well as the moments that have brought you suffering. I can clearly remember someone once told me, "You think about the people you work with more than me." It was the first time anyone had ever challenged me on my desire to help others. I remember feeling deeply hurt by this comment, because at the core of who I am is to help people feel valued and seen. That was the day

I said in my head, *If you do not understand my passion for people, this relationship is never going to work.* From this, my purpose became clearer to me than ever.

I have dedicated my life to ensuring others feel valued both personally and professionally because they thereby have the benefit of an environment where they can experiment and grow. My dedication to developing and valuing others began long before I ever held my first retail job. As an identical twin, I had the joy of a built-in best friend. We shared everything. But as we grew, the differences between us became more and more evident. My mum did not help the situation. She would always say, "Be your own person, love yourself for who you are." This was with good intent to help us embrace our individuality. I heard from an early age not to appreciate being a twin, that it was better to build my own identity. Reading books about twin relationships in my thirties, I learned that being alike is comforting and being together should be celebrated, which I did not experience. As a twin I felt undervalued and not nurtured, and so that is what I learned. I then developed a paralyzing lisp that had a devastating effect on my teen years.

I was mercilessly teased and began to pale in the shadow of my popular twin sister. When I was fifteen, I had mouth surgery and every kind of concoction you can imagine: the train-track braces, the headgear elastics, and all the extras, which in the UK were not very common at the time. Over time, my lisp started to disappear and became not as pronounced as it was previously. My first retail job was in a men's store in the Royal Exchange in Manchester, UK. My manager was an amazing, kind gentleman named Gary, and he taught me how to talk to customers and helped me build my confidence. After a while, I had regular clients who would come to see me and appreciated my fashion and lifestyle advice; what did I know, I was sixteen, but I did listen more than I talked. Because of my lisp, I became an excellent listener and the master of probing questions like, "Tell me more, what do you think?" That first job helped me find my voice. I was living in a new city with a fresh start, without the friends who teased me at school and with a boss who treated me with respect and care and who valued me. Even today, when I look in the mirror, I see my jaw is off-centered, and I have an overbite. This stopped me from public speaking for years and getting on camera. But today, I am proud, value myself, and don't let my self-worth issues overshadow my purpose. Call it age, I am not sure what it is, but when you realize that your job is to help others more than to worry about your own issues, that purpose and influence to encourage and lift others should overtake your lack of self-confidence.

From a young age, my sense of purpose was shrouded by my feeling that I did not have a secure place in the world. Even my relationship with my sister was shaky. I didn't feel valued. What began as a curse soon became a blessing. My struggle to feel valued has continued to fuel my interest in teaching others how to find and function in their purpose. Suffering is a great indicator of growth and life lessons, as long as we view them with this perspective.

What I learned is, my desire to feel valued fueled a passion for helping others feel valued. The feelings of self-doubt that were so familiar to me pushed me to read self-help books and seek ways to overcome those feelings, making me a better leader. I would read books that told me to write positive affirmations and the power of positivity. The funny thing is I have always been positive; positivity has nothing to do with self-worth. Self-worth or self-value is much deeper than that.

Through my quest to become whole and fill the voids within myself, I realized that I was not alone. I realized that working on myself helped me become a better leader to my team. So, for this, I am genuinely grateful. My desire to change those feelings inside myself enabled me to see this in others and ensured my interactions with people never added to their feelings of doubt. If we accept who we are and look deep at the root from which it springs, it allows us to heal. Through our pain, we can create a new outlook or feeling. We can then pass this on to others, which is where the blessing resides.

The question of purpose is crucial to answering in every realm of life. But it becomes even more important in the retail space, where specific challenges arise.

Retail leaders and employees have unique issues to face daily. Retail leaders are not just managers of stores and companies; they are managers of people. But if the leaders of their staff don't operate from a place of purpose and passion, it will have a lasting impact on the success of the business and the people they lead. I have worked for passionate leaders and leaders who are not. The leaders who are driven by their desire to inspire and help others have inspired me to be the best version of myself, which has had a lasting impact on my sense of worth. I remember working for someone who was there for the money and the title rather than how they could add value to others every day. I admired her for her go-getter attitude, but it didn't always feel great being on her team.

Retail managers can easily get lost in the quest to achieve sales targets, recruit and train staff, or manage inventory. Problem-solving (otherwise known as putting out fires) can consume every hour of the day and distract from the absolute joy of management: growing and developing people.

Likewise, employees need to feel a sense of value and purpose in their work. Employees provide customer service in a culture where customers are far more demanding and have many options. Competition is a reality more now than at any other time in retail history. Employees cope with taxing schedules, which compete with family and recreation time. During the holidays, when consumers' days are filled with shopping, retail employees work long hours, often late into the night, on weekends, and on holidays to meet the increased customer demand.

When leaders can cast the vision that the job of retail is much more than "just a job," they can create a dynamic environment where employees feel valued, effective, and motivated, which pours out into the customer service relationship in positive and powerful ways. It is like a ripple in a lake that keeps moving out farther and farther.

An employee who holds positive emotions such as joy, love, desire, happiness, and optimism towards the company, fueled by passion and purpose, has far more impact and delivers stronger results than an employee who receives a pay increase and does not share this same emotion. It will also pour out into their personal life in the way they interact with people. I know this because having these emotions towards my boss and environment has profoundly affected my own life. I discovered my value because I felt valued; I have found my purpose because I uncovered how great I was at helping others; I found out how much I loved teaching others and how to lead. Finding purpose is a lifelong quest for most of us.

Did you know that there are more than one billion Google searches a day asking this question: "How to find my purpose?" This astonishing but not surprising fact reflects our search for meaning in our lives, our own limiting beliefs, and what we have been taught to suppress and value in ourselves. We are continually searching for more. This is human nature.

When I finally acknowledged that my passion was people, I could make a difference by simply treating people on my team with value. I recognized my purpose was to help others learn how to value themselves, by assisting them to see their value-add to the team. Leading with awareness, ACT is not only developing retail skills but life skills. Accepting your purpose is the first step; this can take time, sometimes a lifetime, so do not beat yourself up if you haven't found it yet. The next step is to create the conditions which allow you to live in your purpose. This is not always easy; you may have to make some changes emotionally, and physically it requires being vulnerable. Teaching, coaching, and mentoring others go far beyond the walls of a retail store. The ripple effect on the people you work with will have a lasting impact. Finding purpose is essential to establishing your place in the world. It is the merger of four critical dimensions:

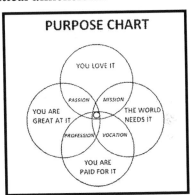

Doing what you love.

Doing something you are good at.

Doing something the world needs and getting paid for it.

The magic occurs in that "little green zone," aka the small center circle, when your skills and passion converge. When you merge all four in one—passion, mission, profession, and vocation—life becomes dynamic and filled with vitality.

If working in retail merges all of these dimensions, consider yourself lucky enough to have found it. If retail does not, then figure out what you like and don't like about it. One thing I love about retail is that it allows me to explore so many different skills. The leaders I have worked for encouraged me to find the one thing I loved and helped me focus on my strengths.

The first time I ever completed assessing my strengths and weaknesses was when I was a district manager; it was so eye-opening. We attended a team retreat, and in advance it was required we complete an online assessment that highlighted our colors and personality communication styles. I learned my need for recognition stopped me from taking risks, which was wrapped up in my lack of self-worth. I also acknowledge that when I hold workshops and have people self-assess their leadership styles, everyone is proud of their strengths and wants the same recognition. This leads me to believe that our desire to feel valued is at the core of all of us and is more profound than we first think.

Confidence is a good disguise for our lack of self-worth; remember this when you lead others. If you can create an environment where each person's skills and abilities are recognized and valued, you will have made a difference to that person. I was having a conversation with a bartender recently who said to me that her passion was bartending, and her family couldn't understand why. They wanted her to go to school and get a formal education etc.

She looked me dead in the eye and said, "When I get asked how I will change the world serving people drinks, I say, 'one person at a time.' I get to help people feel good, and they tell me their life stories. They talk to me about their bosses, their spouses, and what kind of day they had. I get to listen, be there, and create a fun environment. I have clients who follow me from restaurant to restaurant, because I help them have a piece of happiness in their day."

If you have ever googled, "what is my purpose" or "how to find purpose," then I would ask you to look at what you love doing. Finding your purpose could be as simple as encouraging others, inspiring others, helping others develop into a leader when they thought they were just a stock person or cashier. Your purpose does not have to be bigger than that. For a long time, I did not identify myself working in retail as being purposeful. I saw it as a job. Your purpose in retail may be as simple as to empower others. So many people work in retail as a part-time job, but what they can learn and gain from a retail manager is much more than just folding clothes, as long as you see yourself this way. Maybe you love to stand up for people who can't speak for themselves. Perhaps you love to coach and develop, or maybe you love to help people feel valued. Whatever your passion is and what makes you *love* leading a team is most likely your purpose. When you ignite this in yourself, you will see that your passion for helping people is purposeful.

Many people I have worked with had terrible home lives or were alone. They felt that their retail family was their family. They felt that they could talk to their retail family more than their actual family. Retail leaders are more than just managers; they are there for people over and over again. When you care for people, you have the highest calling of anyone on this planet, in my book! So, don't ever think you don't have a purpose working retail, and you have nothing of value. *You* have a *huge* purpose to lift, inspire, encourage, motivate, teach, accept and value people.

CHAPTER 6

Valuing Others

A Life Lesson

Don't take for granted the one thing you think is easy. It's your unique gift. Value it, polish it, and then share it with others. Your value is not based on net worth—your value is based on self-worth.

AS WE'VE DISCUSSED, THE "A" in ACT means to *accept*. When we first accept ourselves, it means we value ourselves. When we do this, we can then accept others for who they are and show them we support and value their unique strengths and weaknesses, which is empowering. When people feel valued, they step into their personal power, which ultimately makes a better environment for work and their personal lives. In a recent Gallup survey, only 20 percent of all employees are actively engaged and happy in their jobs. But what if we could change this by doing one simple thing: valuing them?

In my opinion, it is every leader's biggest responsibility to make each person on their team feel valued. Working to foster a culture where employees feel valued is something I have committed to throughout my professional life. Why? Because it's critical in business to find meaning in all the environments where we invest our time. In return, those people build businesses.

But, what does it mean to value others? And why is it important in retail? The first lesson of valuing others in business is realizing that employees who feel valued, listened to, and encouraged deliver measurably better results.

The act of valuing others is quite simple. By adhering to some simple guidelines, you can ensure that the people who work with you know that you recognize their worth.

See People

Like … really see them. The people we work with are real people. They come with the same issues, loves, joys, pains, and fears as everyone else. Showing compassion ensures that you see the people you manage as whole individuals, not just worker bees hired to accomplish a business goal. Showing compassion means caring about the individuals on your team as well as the team as a whole. It also means valuing their work experience as highly as you value their work product. Many people on your team may have previous work experience and life experience that could add value or perspective to their current projects or roles. When you ignore this and act as if what they did before doesn't matter, you are not demonstrating an interest in them. Some managers feel threatened by people on their team. Don't let this be you. Let people know that you value their experience by asking them their opinions and perspectives on certain situations and ask them to share any experiences they have had that could help the current situation. Many people in retail have had other careers and come with a wealth of skills and abilities. For example, I have worked with teachers, project managers, nurses, event coordinators; the list goes on. These experiences, when allowed to be expressed, aid the team as a whole.

Listen and Learn

Another meaningful way to communicate to people how much we value them is to listen. It's easy for managers to do all the talking and to be directing orders to their subordinates.

But the retail staff on the front lines have a unique and important perspective about the inner workings of our businesses that managers need to consider. Without assumption or interruption, listening helps employees feel respected and may have the added benefit of teaching managers something about the business they did not know.

Your team needs your most empathetic and truest listening to signal that they have worth in your organization. It is essential not to skip past what they are trying to tell you. Some managers barely look up from their desks when their employees try to talk to them. Or, worse, some managers carry on conversations as they walk by without ever stopping to look at their employees eye-to-eye. This creates a disconnection.

This is difficult. Just recently, I was in a situation where I witnessed how a manager can miss what his or her employee is really trying to say. I pointed it out directly to the manager, who acknowledged that he did not see what I saw. His focus was on what he needed to do, and he was oblivious to the employee in front of him. Sometimes you will need to listen to what is being said while acutely aware of what is not being said. This is precisely what I witnessed. I was sitting with the manager when he called another department to let a man named Johnathan know that he wanted to speak with him right before leaving for the day. As it was not Johnathan that answered the call, he asked Gen to pass on the message and said, "Hi, Gen, can you ask Johnathan to come and see me right before he leaves for the day? Thanks so much." After about five minutes, Johnathan appeared in the manager's office. The manager looked surprised and then proceeded to say, "I am not ready for you now. Can you come back? I asked Gen to tell you to come to see me right before you leave for the day."

Looking confused, Johnathan responded, "This has been happening to me all day; every time I try and get my job done, I get asked to go and do something for someone." The manager said, "Ok, well, me too. So, can you come back later?" When Johnathan left the room, the manager turned to me and said, "Nobody listens to me. I asked him to come and see me before he left."

I am sure, at face value, this sounds like a typical interaction that could happen many times throughout the day. The manager and Johnathan got along well, so there wasn't much damage done. They were able to return to smiling and joking with each other.

Can you imagine how much more effective the manager would have been if he had said, "Hi, Gen, can you ask Johnathan what time he finishes today and then call me back?" Gen might have called back and said, "He's here for another three hours—until about seven." Then the manager could have said, "Great, can you ask him to come and see me at six forty-five? I have a few things I would like to discuss with him before he leaves."

Even in the scenario where there was a miscommunication between the manager and Gen, the manager could have taken the path of empathy and said, "Johnathan, I am so sorry to hear that you have been pulled away all day from your job. I know how frustrating that can be. I was not specific enough and should have asked what time you were leaving. I value your time and know that you are working hard. How about you let me know fifteen minutes before you're leaving, and I will come and see you? Thank you for prioritizing me."

Even though it was not terrible, the scenario that happened did not show Johnathan he was valued. If this keeps happening, as small as it seems, it will wear Johnathan down slowly like water dripping on a stone. It will eventually erode his morale. After a couple of months, he may become fed up and leave. The manager will assume he left for more money, which is what I hear all the time from managers. But in reality, he left because his worth was not evident to management. It has been said that people will work for money, but they will die for recognition. Valuing others takes effort. Listening takes an effort to hear what's being said and what's not being said.

Ask Questions and Lots of Them

Asking questions is a skill. Most managers ask questions with the answer already in their minds. Think about this, and be honest with yourself. Are you truly curious? Do you really want to know what someone thinks? Or are you asking questions with the outcome in mind? You may not want to admit this. I can think of many circumstances where I have had pre-meetings. This is called getting aligned, which means figuring out how to influence or manipulate the participants to get the outcome we want. The problem with this method is it values only one opinion: *yours.* When you value others' perspectives and contributions, you will ask open questions to discover and uncover what a person really thinks; you will be focused and present. You will be so comfortable with the unknown that it won't matter what the answer is; instead, you will value what your team is saying, and they will know it. It's a nonverbal way of saying, I hear and see you!

I can remember when I was a store manager, and my district manager had me prepare in advance what I was going to say and what not to say to the questions she was going to ask during a corporate visit. I was so confused by this; I thought it was such a waste of time. I also felt that she didn't trust and value me.

Even though I ran a twenty-million-dollar store, the visitors came and left, and the visit went well, in her opinion. In mine, it went terribly, because they didn't know the real struggles we faced, what we needed to improve the results and gain the help to overcome these challenges. I vowed that if I ever became a senior leader, I would visit stores and never make managers feel like this. I ask questions to learn, and I don't judge people by "how" they tell me; I listen for what they are telling me. I have studied the art of asking open-ended questions.

The book, *Ask Powerful Questions*, by Will Wise, is one of the best books I have read on questioning. In this book, he talks about the power of asking the right questions, and he shares that most people ask questions that are leading because they want to be right. And the opposite of being open is being right, not closed as most people would think. Leaders who ask questions intending to guide the conversation are actually manipulating the situation. He also says that most people are not comfortable with the unknown. This is so true. If you are listening to learn, you are very comfortable with the unknown; you cannot learn from a place of all-knowing. The next time you engage in a conversation, observe yourself and see if your questioning is leading someone or if you are truly curious about what the other person is saying. If you think and say, "I know the answer," or "That's not right," you are not listening to learn.

When I work with senior teams trying to solve issues for their customers, I always remind them that the answers are all in the field. This is a critical perspective to keep in mind. Be aware; if you ask the field operators a question, you will have to be open to the answers and then be prepared to do something with the information being presented. If you do not, then the feedback will feel like it has no value, which ultimately means the team giving it has no value. So, if you're going to ask, find ways to address the feedback; even if you respond that you cannot take action today, say it.

Make It About Them—Not You.

People are masters at evaluating other people, even if only on a subconscious level. Even as babies, we know how to read facial expressions. Dr. Williams Sears of *Parenting* magazine states that babies can even pick up on their parent's anxiety and choose not to be held by someone their parents don't like. People know when you care about what matters to them and respond to it on a visceral level.

Unfortunately, it is not easy to develop the habit of putting others first. We are hardwired for self-preservation. But self-preservation doesn't have to be selfish. The best managers are the ones who put the needs of the team before their own. In Les Giblin's book, *Skill with People*, he shares how human nature is more interested in ourselves than anyone else. And he says that when you know this, you can work with human nature instead of against it. When you embrace this truth, your team will buy into your leadership. This extra effort comes intrinsically and is not something you can pay for. John C. Maxwell says, "Go and work for a not-for-profit," and find out if you can get people to work for you. Then you will learn this simple but effective perspective.

Furthermore, it goes without saying that without people, you don't have a business. You cannot do it alone. You cannot open a retail store without a team. You cannot provide excellent customer service unless you have people who love what they do and are enthusiastic about keeping customers coming back.

Encourage Others to Share Ideas No Matter How Small

You never know what the next million-dollar idea might be or the idea that saves money, time, and effort. For example, Audi solicited employee suggestions. The following year, Audi reported a savings of $40 million (€33 million) in its Győr and Brussels plants as a result of implementing ideas from the 10,100 employee suggestions they received. In a *Harvard Business Review* report, researcher David Burkus writes, "The researchers found that the creativity of front-line service employees (which they called 'service creativity') directly affected customer service ratings. "Service creativity allows employees to delight customers in unusual ways or solve problems that existing protocol falls short of addressing," said Jing Zhou, a co-author of the study and professor of management at Rice University.

> *"The findings suggest that service creativity is a powerful avenue through which customer satisfaction can be achieved."* Jing Zhou

When I worked as a store manager at Starbucks in Florida, we wanted more than anything for our customers to pick up the right drink at the end of the line. As my store was on South Beach and our customers were tourists on vacation, they didn't pay attention to what they had ordered or picked up at the end of the bar. This was an ongoing issue. During conference calls and soliciting feedback from the team, we came up with the idea to put the name on the cup so that every person got the right drink. This didn't cost the company any money. A simple question, "What's your name?" was born, and every customer got what they ordered. Little did we know that it would become the international standard at the time. I learned a valuable lesson: listening to ideas, small and big, can make a huge impact.

When I joined Starbucks UK, I had come from working at the Gap, where we had a zone chart and floor plan to ensure that everyone was in the right place at the right time. I took this concept and applied it to Starbucks. I created a map and called it a slide deployment map that assigned your primary and secondary roles on shift. It helped my team stay on top of customer service and stay organized. I made sure that everyone was in the right place at the right time. This was over twenty years ago; it was a simple idea, a whiteboard in the back room with a store map on it. The store I was in most recently had that map on the backroom wall; I saw it when their door was open. This made me realize that, again, small ideas can make a big difference.

When I was standing looking at this map recently, it took me back to when I had one of the best bosses I have ever had in my career. I was new to the district and America.

She created a place where I could share my ideas and was open-minded. She always made me feel my ideas were valuable and allowed me to try things out. She helped my self-worth by valuing what I had to offer. It's incredible what a boss like this can do for you; not only had I been able to implement two ideas that are still very much alive today, but she added steam to my self-esteem. She encouraged and helped me have a voice that was heard in my district and the larger network. I have been fortunate to have leaders like this in my career that enabled me to find my self-worth by valuing my ideas, voice, and contribution. I found her on LinkedIn recently and thanked her for encouraging me to share my ideas and valuing them. She had a massive part in building my confidence as a leader and a woman.

Give the gift of your time. One word that is synonymous with retail life is speed. Everything moves at a rapid pace. But it is essential to stop occasionally and spend time with your team. Slow down and be present; this is extremely hard now that we all have iPhones and are wired up all day to results and email.

The time spent talking and listening to your team will drive the rest of the retail day and improve efficiency overall. You might also want to consider taking the time for team members who may not report directly to you but rather facilitate open conversation cross-functionally. This builds a creative culture where ideas are safe to surface.

Even though most offices are open plan these days, there are still far too many silos. We'll explore this more later. Knowing how to build collaboration is something most retailers struggle with, as field operators and head office roles are so different and complex to understand from both sides of the fence. Slowing down enough to be present and give someone your time is valuable. And equally valuable is asking someone to do the same, so make sure you value people's time as you do your own. I have seen many examples of this, not just in retail, in life, and I am guilty of this with my children.

I am so focused on work and being the provider; I missed moments where I could have been more present. Now as they get older, I realize that time is a commodity and one you cannot get back. We find it easy to give customers our time because we are gaining something, a sale. But what if you had nothing to gain? Would you still give your time? We would all like to say yes, but everything we do is to benefit ourselves if we are truly honest with ourselves. This is normal. Time is the most valuable commodity, and when you give it genuinely, it shows you care, making others feel valued. It's not difficult to give of yourself. The only costs are your effort, awareness, and thinking of others before yourself. When we offer time to each other, we create collaborative space that we would not gain if we were rushing around all day. When we are relaxed and in a state of connection, our brains can create. To allow this to happen, we must listen to others and make the time.

Use the Power of Recognition

When people are recognized for their contributions, it makes them feel valued. Humans crave recognition. A powerful way to ensure your team knows their value is to recognize them for their efforts, both big and small. While reading a relationship book called *The Five Love*

Languages, I learned that my love language is words of affirmation. Having self-worth issues, I can relate to why I needed this. As I grew in my leadership, age and confidence, I didn't need it as much anymore.

I remember when I was recruited for a multi-store role. It would be my first district manager position, and I was nervous about leaving my team and the comfort of what I knew. I called an old boss to ask for advice. She shared her words of wisdom with me:

> *Once you work in multi-site, you will no longer receive*
> *feedback daily and recognition; so, if you're ready to let*
> *go of this, then you're ready to grow into a multi-site role.*

The other wisdom she gave me was to set up a folder called positive feedback in my outlook. When I received great compliments or positive feedback emails, file them so that, from time to time, if I needed validation to lift myself, I could go into that folder and read them. This folder has been with me for over fifteen years now. For someone who thrives on positive feedback and recognition, it fuels me to keep these emails and remind myself of my value from time to time. When you recognize people, it tells them you see them, and when you see them, it sends a message of value that reaches their core.

Valuing people comes down to showing people (rather than just saying to people) that you care. Don't take them for granted. As the old saying goes, "people don't care how much you know until they know how much you care." It is far more essential to build culture first and strategy second. You get a higher level of buy-in when you allow your team to help craft the organization's strategy.

Team members who function at the level of purpose help everyone on the team feel appreciated every day. It's not just a manager-to-employee effect. When employees feel that they are valuable team members, they offer the same positivity to those around them. I've heard horror stories, as I'm sure you have, of work environments where employees feel like nothing more than a number, a bother, or a subordinate. People may show up to the company every day, but they never fully invest themselves and give their all until they know that they matter.

If you have not included a recognition program for your people as part of your strategic action plan, then you might want to think about this. Part of your plan should consist of actions and a focus on ensuring your people feel valued and recognized; if they do not, your people may already be actively looking for another job. A leader I worked with told me, "Just because you're not focused on culture doesn't mean you don't have one; every business has a culture. It just might not be the one you want." This is a compelling thought and one that should be taken seriously. Goals and results are indeed important, but without motivated, engaged, and valued employees, the results will not be significant or long-lasting.

CHAPTER 7

Leading Yourself

A Life Lesson

You must lead yourself before you can lead others.

LEADING YOURSELF IS A REVOLUTIONARY concept in management. Great leaders do much more than lead great teams; they lead themselves, motivate themselves, and inspire themselves to grow. There are many strategies managers can use to lead themselves.

In my career, I've learned much: how to manage through change, how to overcome adversity, and how to stay connected to the people who matter.

I am fortunate to wake up every day and do something that electrifies and inspires me. Today my favorite thing to do is work in a store and talk with team members and customers. Whenever I get the chance to work in-store, it reminds me of my days managing one. When I am in-store, I get to serve others, which I believe we are all here to do in some form or capacity. The best way I can describe it for me is, I get to be mindful of others' needs versus my own, which I find truly rewarding. That said, I know it was my commitment to grow and improve that allowed me to invest in the growth of others. It's very easy when leading others to forget to spend time working on yourself.

Take Care of Yourself Spiritually

When I moved to Toronto, it was one of the most difficult times for me personally. I left a team I loved working with. The company transferred me, on my request, as it was a personal decision I had to make at the time to put some distance between myself and my son's father. I was fortunate enough to have a company and leaders who supported me and put me on an assignment in Toronto. My best friend from the UK had relocated to Canada. Moving close to her would provide me with some support for myself and my children.

I was doing exceptionally well at work but not in my personal life. I was a single mum of two kids and had gone through a bad breakup. I needed to heal. As I mentioned earlier, I met someone who took me to a Buddhist meditation practice on Bathurst Street. He said he went there to de-stress and that this is something I might want to consider. I was searching for myself after losing myself amid the move and breakup. My work and team were amazing, and I wanted to be the best person I could be for them and my kids. So, I decided to try meditation. It was not easy, but with practice I found it helped me tremendously. Now, fifteen years later, every Thursday evening, I head to a Buddhist temple in downtown Toronto to meditate. I love it! It's a place in the city where I can spend time practicing the art of mindfulness (which means reaching a mental state by focusing one's awareness on the present moment). I would say that mindfulness has made me better in many ways. One of the most significant benefits is that I am a better listener and more present, which helps me deal with what is in front of me at any given moment. It has also made me aware of my feelings as a logical leader and thinker. I am in my head a lot of the time, which works for me in leadership; however, this does not work so much in relationships and with my kids, where they need me to be more emotional.

You are mind, body, and spirit. We take part in many activities that challenge and grow our minds, and many of us have embraced the importance of regular physical exercise. But spiritual care is a critical component that completes the mystical package which encompasses our makeup. Vedic educator Rachelle Williams says,

> *Perhaps your concept of spirituality is experienced in nature, in one another, or within oneself. It could be through art, music, and dance. Ultimately, it can be anything that is meaningful and kindles a sense of sacredness, even if only felt by you. Spirituality is a personal practice. No matter what path is chosen, they all converge upon something you desire on some level—the need for connection, purpose, and happiness. A spiritual self-care practice is any ritual that connects you to your true self, the real you. The real you is the raw expression of who you were meant to be and offer this world. It's energizing, inspiring, and, most of all, it feels right. Perhaps you already are experiencing this or maybe have had glimpses of what this might look or feel like. Becoming familiar with how you feel is an essential part of being able to navigate through life. Accessing that part of yourself through spiritual self-care can be rewarding on many levels.*

One way to achieve spiritual self-care is through the practice of meditation. Meditation is a powerful way to grow your mind and calm your spirit. Many leadership books introduce the concept of mindfulness into the workplace. Mindfulness is an ancient tradition in Buddhism. It not only teaches you to be present but also awakens you to understand that nothing is permanent. You learn how to appreciate this. When you can accept the impermanence of life, you will become more at peace. Think about it—each wave that crashes in the ocean is unique. That same wave has never appeared before, and the ocean will never create the same wave again.

When you can integrate this thinking into your leadership, you will take things less personally. This freedom of thought allows others to be themselves. The one constant in life is change. Being more mindful and less attached will help you navigate change easily. In today's retail world, this skill is critical to leaders and managers as they lead people and the business.

One of my favorite books is *The Science of Mind*, by Ernest Holmes. This is an ancient teaching; it is one that is still relevant today. It is the basis of how I lead and live my life. The foundation of his teachings is the universal law of cause and effect. If this law is true, looking after our body, mind, and spirit should be something that every leader considers. Being a leader in self-care is essential. A good example of this is on an airplane. If the mask drops, you are supposed to put it on your face first before helping others. Why? Because you have to be alive to save another person's life.

In a conversation with my son recently, we were reflecting on last year's visioning we had done together and the power of our minds using positive affirmations. I will share more about this later in the book, as I believe our minds are the most powerful tool we have, and they should be treated as such. Spiritual development and growth were genuine gifts my mother gave me. She would send me books on this topic and discuss spiritual ideas with me. This has helped me lead myself and therefore lead others from a bigger perspective.

Show Yourself Empathy

We will explore empathy at greater length in the next chapter. But suffice it to say that we have become experts at beating ourselves up.

But just as you must learn to offer empathy to those who work on your team, you must also extend empathy to yourself. It's vital to admit fault when you miscalculate or make mistakes, but the practice of holding on to errors, whether intentional or unintentional, is emotionally unhealthy and bad for business.

Intentional acts like losing your temper or making selfish choices are serious errors. It's important to acknowledge the mistake, learn all you can from it, and move on. Psychologists tell us that it can become a mechanism that stops us from accepting responsibility, seeking forgiveness, and making amends when we beat ourselves up. Unintentional mistakes are a necessary part of corporate life. Mistakes help us to understand what doesn't work and to move on more effectively. Mistakes also help us identify gaps in our knowledge, but harping on mistakes drains us of the energy we need to move forward. Learning to respond versus react as a leader is an essential quality.

Dr. Rick Hanson, psychologist and *New York Times* best-selling author, says:

> *It's one thing to call yourself to task for a fault, try to understand what caused it, resolve to correct it, act accordingly, and move on. This is psychologically healthy and morally accountable. It's another matter entirely to grind on yourself, to lambaste your own character, to fasten on the negative and ignore the good in you, to find yourself wanting – in other words, to beat yourself up. This excessive inner criticism tears you down instead of building your strengths; it's stressful and thus wears on your mood, health, and longevity.*

Become a Lifelong Learner

Growing as a leader cannot be overstated. While your past training and experiences have served you well in getting to your current position, there is still more to learn. Books, conferences, and courses are great tools to help you broaden your bandwidth as a leader and expose you to trends and concepts you may not yet be aware of. Performance strategist and Mayberry Enterprises CEO, Matt Mayberry, wrote this in an article for entrepreneur.com:

> *Much success is derived from highly motivated individuals that have dedicated their lives to the concept of lifelong learning. These individuals prioritize the creation of time in their busy lives each day to educate themselves on new concepts and ideas. In an ever-changing market and world, it's more important than ever to stay current, competitive, and up to date. First and foremost, you must be willing to expand your mind. Rid yourself of assumptions and convictions so that you can be open and receptive to new information.*

> *This, at times, may even contradict what you have always believed to be true. You will eventually come across information that challenges your worldview.*

> *Rather than remaining static in your comfort zone, use this time to stop, reflect and shed light on these ideas in a way that can develop and expand your vision. When you come across new information, take the time to think about what you believe and why. Is your outdated mindset preventing you from advancing in a modern world?*

I have dedicated myself to learning. When I was about ten years into my retail career, I thought I had enough information and experience to apply in other businesses. You cannot copy and paste what you have previously learned into every new situation, because when you do this, you become an expert on only a few things. When I became a John C. Maxwell coach in 2014, I discovered that being a lifelong learner ensures that I serve well the teams and businesses I work in. When I worked at Apple, I was always amazed at how much information the specialists on the sales floor could remember. One of the best qualities, in my opinion, was the desire to learn new technology. Innovative products will do that to you. Treat your brain like a new computer, and think about what you are doing with it every day. Do you have a personal development plan for growth? If not, why not? Learning is so easy in today's world of TED talks, blog posts, and podcasts. Make it your mission to learn something and then share it. This is ACT in action.

Leading yourself means offering yourself the same level of care and concern you hope to provide for your team. It means listening to your body when it says it needs to rest. It means eating healthy and exercising. It means taking time to grow and develop the skills you need to move to the next level. It means loving and caring for you!

CHAPTER 8

The Power of Empathy

A Life Lesson

Feeling understood and heard is a basic human need.

EMPATHY AND COMPASSION ARE TWO of my favorite words. Empathy is not characterized by weakness in leadership; it's a strength. I was fortunate to have a senior executive tell me this over twelve years ago, and it was the best advice I've ever received. Empathy and compassion are key EI (emotional intelligence) competencies. If you don't develop them, you will never work well with others.

Have you ever seen a question about empathy pop up on a performance review? I would wager you haven't. Yet, empathy is a gift we all wish to receive from the people we come into contact with. Empathy, the ability to put yourself in another person's shoes, allows you to connect with people on a deeper level. Empathy fosters trust and builds bulletproof relationships.

You've heard the phrase, "Treat others how you want to be treated." It's the famous Golden Rule. But it can go even further. As it is called, the Platinum Rule suggests that you treat people how they want to be treated. In other words, tap into every person's uniqueness and provide them with the experience that would be most fitting to them.

According to *Psychology Today,*

> *Empathy is the visceral experience of another*
> *person's thoughts and feelings from his or her*
> *point of view, rather than from one's own.*

> *Empathy facilitates prosocial or helping behaviors*
> *that come from within, rather than being forced, so*
> *that people behave in a more compassionate manner.*
> *Empathy stands in contrast to sympathy, which is the*
> *ability to cognitively understand a person's point of*
> *view or experience without the emotional overlay.*

That's where empathy begins. It calls you away from inwardly focused thoughts and activities and lures you to a higher place of outward focus. In the workplace, empathy is often relegated to a place of emotionalism or softness. We have been conditioned to remove emotions and feelings from the work environment. The truth is that great strength is required to display empathy in business.

We may surmise that empathy is a difficult emotion to muster; in reality, it is a natural instinct that we are conditioned to numb from years of suppression.

There are many techniques we can employ to reawaken our sense of empathy:

> *Put aside your viewpoint and try to see things from the*
> *other person's point of view.*

While focusing on others is a challenge in our me-focused society, it becomes more natural when setting aside your viewpoint. This requires a level of intentionality you may not have used since childhood. Employees who feel that you hear them and understand their side are more likely to work with you towards a goal or solve a problem. One of my favorite activities to do with leaders is to have them practice this exercise. For at least twenty-four hours (or as long as you can), take out *I*, *me*, *my*, and *mine* from your vocabulary when communicating with others, whether that comes in the form of spoken or written communication. Once I asked a leader to complete this, because she rubbed her team the wrong way (against human nature). She said it took her three days to write an email to her team. It was so difficult, but she learned a lot. If you have never tried this, go ahead, and see how long you last.

Validate the Other Person's Perspective

Author and leader Stephen R. Covey famously said, "First seek to understand, then to be understood." The human psyche craves validation. It transcends gender, age, culture, and geography. It is part of our makeup as humans to feel connected to others via their acceptance of us. This is the first step in leading with awareness, ACT: *acceptance* is key. By validating the other person's perspective, we are not making a value judgment. We are not saying they are right or wrong. We are merely saying, "I want to understand what you are saying and how this situation is making you feel." Some key phrases you can say that will help you get there are:

- Thank you for pointing that out.
- Tell me more about that.
- You have every right to feel that way.
- Is there anything else you want to share?

Leaders become great leaders when they learn to accept people on their teams for who they are rather than who they want them to be. The truth is that if we had experienced the other person's background, upbringing, parents, and life experiences, we might feel exactly as they do. So, the ability to accept their point of view is a marker of growth in leadership.

Examine Your Attitude

Are you more concerned with how you are impacted by an employee's behavior than what caused that employee's behavior? An attitude of self-preservation tempts us to protect ourselves from criticism or anger. We tend to focus on what is important to us and emphasize four potentially dangerous words: "*I, me, my,* and *mine.*" Instead, replace a conversation about yourself with a conversation about your team. Use the words "you," "your," and "we" more often. Surrender the satisfaction you can get from talking about yourself. You will find that your influence will be significantly increased. Hold others in positive regard always. This may sound counterintuitive to those skeptics out there, but it's natural for those of us who are eternal optimists. I had a fantastic boss who was more skeptical than me; I loved it when you put us together; we were balanced and could always meet in the middle. Having a positive, optimistic attitude will encourage others to share more of the same.

Listen

Leaders are usually great communicators—at least, they are great with half of the communication cycle: the talking. The other part of communication involves listening. Leaders that can communicate from the outside and focus on others rather than themselves are very influential. Motivational speaker and *New York Times* bestselling author Robyn Benincasa says:

> *A powerful step that leaders can take to improve their impact is to gain a deep understanding of the employee experience. What's really happening on the shop floor? What are the greatest barriers that employees encounter when undertaking projects? What do team members genuinely need in terms of support, tools, and resources? What do they think and*

feel about coming to work each day? What are they excited about, and what gets in their way? Listening can help leaders expand their understanding and make a positive impact on culture. If better listening helps retain key employees, improves morale, builds trust, and increases engagement, no further justification is required. No one person, including executives, has all the answers. Employees are savvy and can see through empty statements, fluffy platitudes, and messages that fail to align with their personal experiences on the job. If your goal is to improve and grow your organization, become known as an authentic leader who understands that delivering strong business results first requires building strong professional relationships. Listening expands perspectives and enables an organization to proactively address potential issues rather than simply react to them after they escalate."

This is why I find it fascinating when companies do not hold employee net-promoter surveys with their entire population. If people like to be heard, why wouldn't you want to embrace this idea and ask your employees how they feel about working for you?

For the first ten years of my retail career, I was measured on people's opinions of how they felt about working for me. Trust me; when your annual appraisal considers this, and you are measured on how engaged your team is, you will think carefully and work hard to listen to your team. Even in tough conversations, you will strive to communicate and ensure your team feels heard.

Leadership creates culture; ACT, leading with awareness, is about creating the conditions to make this real.

Apple is a master of this, so it's no surprise that its culture is positive when leaders are held responsible for how the team feels. This has a direct impact on recruitment and customer service. When your team feels listened to and heard, magic happens in your store, and this can transform a dying brand into a top performer all over again.

Ask the other person what they would do. When you aren't sure what the other person wants or needs, ask. Making assumptions about another person's feelings or expectations is dangerous. We all view situations differently and can be impacted by our experiences in a thousand different ways. It's important not to assume people see an issue the same way you see it. Asking questions like:

- What do you think would help the situation?
- How have you handled situations like this in the past?
- What resolution would you be most comfortable with?
- How would you like the situation to be resolved?
- What would you do?

These are beneficial to ask. Demonstrating the first step of ACT, leading with awareness stops us from making assumptions and judgments; it guides us to accept others' reality, not just our own. To show empathy, you must be curious about others. This can be considered a leadership superpower, and for those, you lead.

CHAPTER 9

Mindful Leadership

A Life Lesson

*Sitting in meditation for thirty minutes a day
is the most valuable time of your day.*

MINDFUL LEADERSHIP IS THE PATH to becoming a conscious leader—conscious of yourself, your employees, your customers, and the impact of your work in the world. The universe brings you more of what you give. I have been fortunate to learn this lesson early in my life through different experiences. It is much like planting seeds in the ground—you will reap what you sow. If you think you can get ahead by ignoring and taking advantage of others, think again. That is a very superficial thought process. If you have had this mindset in the past, now is the time to think bigger and beyond.

A mentor told me about five years ago that making money is easy, but making money while doing the right thing is difficult. If you have a vision for your life, ask yourself if your vision includes and, more importantly, benefits others. If not, it's time to reimagine your role as a leader. Mindfulness equals a level of selflessness and paying attention to who and what are around you. Think about this on the level of what you do with your time, energy, and money. My best friend and I decided that every time we wanted to buy something for ourselves, like a new pair of shoes or something that we didn't need, we would stop and transfer the amount to a savings account and then donate it at the end of thirty days. This kind of mindfulness will change your perspective. Get a group of leaders together and set your intention to do something together for thirty days; a shared mindful experience can have a powerful effect. It will also bring awareness to your leadership.

Your mind is churning all day long with thoughts about who you are in relation to those around you and what you want to be. Pay attention to those thoughts and feelings. If they are not positive images of ways you can help, inspire, encourage, and enhance others, it may be time to work on your paradigms and subject them to a massive shift.

Here's a great mindful practice to get you started:

Take 15 minutes right now, sit back, rub the tips of your middle finger and thumb together very slightly, and connect with your thoughts. Allow them to roam free. Allow your concerns to flow alongside your joys. Free your mind to release both the things that excite you and the things that you fear.

Another great way to become more mindful is to start a journal and write down two things weekly that you did to be more selfless. If it's hard for you at first, that's ok. Just stick with it for thirty days, and see your paradigms shift.

Seizing Authenticity

We live in a world filled with beauty, glorious sunsets, majestic mountain ranges, sleepy meadows beside quiet streams. But we also live in a world that offers us immense amounts of artificiality: virtual friendships, plastic surgery, and fads that go as fast as they come.

The things considered most beautiful to us are those that are authentic ... things that are real. Being authentic means living in truth and embracing honesty about who you are. ACT or being authentic is the highest form of leadership. In so doing, we free our employees to be fully authentic as well.

Leading with Emotion

People are full of emotions, and that's a great thing. Every organization wants customers to have the best experience. And because of this, they hire managers and team members who are masters at building strong relationships. When strong bonds have formed, it creates a fun and engaging place to work and shop. It's what fuels customer service and sales. Customers need to like and feel comfortable in the store for them to make a purchase. It can become a challenge for managers when we have formed good relationships with our teams and now must approach a tough conversation. Nobody likes having performance conversations. Let's face it—it's not our favorite part of the job. However, it can be one of the most rewarding things you do once you master the art of doing it and changing the way you look at it.

Denying emotions means denying the essence of your teams, your customers, and yourself. People experience a wide range of emotions throughout the day. Those emotions are what help to guide them in their interactions. If you can tap into that emotional side of yourself, you will form longlasting connections with everyone on your team. We need to learn how to curb our emotions to make neutral decisions; logic and reason must kick in during these situations. However, don't be afraid to embrace your emotional side and let your team see that part of you. Being human is important and a part of connecting the hearts and minds of those that work with you.

I learned this with my team in Miami. I had been looking after a store as an interim store manager, and when it was time for me to complete the assignment, the team presented me with a poem. I still have it. I was so shocked when they presented it. I had no idea they felt this way. It made me tear up, which I had never done in my entire career in front of my team. The next day, I received a promotion and took on that team permanently before moving to Canada. I learned that connecting the hearts and minds of those around you is a powerful thing, and it's ok to feel emotions as a leader. Being a mindful leader is understanding this so that you can motivate and engage those around you. Mindfulness is mastered when you intentionally put your team first and help them feel they are the most important people in the world.

Resist Personal Biases

Do you overlook people's performance issues because you value what they do well, or ignore small matters for fear of demotivating them? If this sounds familiar, it is most likely because you allow your personal biases to get in the way. Don't worry—you are not alone. This is normal. Having tough, honest conversations is not natural for most of us, never mind for those who work at being in service to customers and our teams every day. Most managers weigh out the good versus the bad and place value on team members' positive skills and strengths. The problem with this is that high performers with bad attitudes can affect the team. Also, inconsistent performers can have a negative impact on the whole team. Ensure you are not overplacing value on the wrong things, letting behaviors slide, and giving too many chances.

Follow Up Frequently

Lack of follow-up with team members when they are not meeting expectations is like boiling water in a kettle. It will eventually blow! It is difficult to follow up on poor performers when you have not been clear with the expectations upfront.

Reflect on this for a moment; how good are you at being clear and direct with your team? Go back to the point above and ask yourself why that is. It could be that you have so much going on and maybe are overwhelmed, or you just don't make time. Or, it could be that you value the wrong things and therefore let things slide. Whatever your reasons are, lack of follow-up will derail your team from reaching their highest potential. Following up on good performance is just as important as following up on underperforming team members. Do your employees know what you expect of them? Or are they running around from crisis to crisis or worse, trying to look busy so as not to incur your rage?

The old paradigms of leadership will not work in the current culture. They probably never did work very well. It is necessary to learn and develop skills that allow you to hold the most productive performance conversations with your team as you guide them toward greater and greater success.

Ultimately, we want you to get the most from your team and manage your time so you can spend more time doing what you love most: helping customers, developing talent, and ensuring you are driving results, making bonuses, and progressing your retail career.

I read a lot about mindfulness in leadership books in which the authors introduce meditation and being present. This is crucial; I also believe being a mindful leader is how you communicate to your team when they are not performing. This is one of the areas where most leaders I work with struggle. The most recent book I have read on mindfulness is *The Mind of a Leader*, by Jaqueline Carter and Rasmus Hougard. It's brilliant because it breaks down empathy and the dangers of being too empathetic.

Being a mindful leader means being aware and present with what is happening, being mindful of your responsibility towards others, and being honest with your people to help them grow. When you can hold conscious performance conversations, you will master leading with awareness.

Helping others and probing into their future career and growth within the current organization is your role. Supporting team members to become aware that their current choice is not working for them, to self-select to pursue other opportunities, is mindfulness at its best.

To practice being more mindful when you're out in public places, sit back and listen, put down your phone, pay attention to the people around you and what people are saying. I like to exercise this in airports, because I don't know the people around me. I like to observe, sit back, and practice listening to how others are connecting. It is fascinating to me because it puts me in a mindful moment. What I mean by this is I can be present and conscious of what's going on around me and listen to other stories. I have nobody to talk to about *me*. I am merely a passenger going to a destination who could be anyone. When I am on the plane, I practice speaking with the passengers sitting next to me. I like to make it a game to find out as much about them as possible while not sharing much about me. I answer questions when they ask me; however, I make the conversation all about them and practice my listening skills.

Try this the next time you are traveling, even if it's on a train. My business partner always finds it amusing that I meet the most interesting people and have made many new contacts and connections while traveling. I think it's because I listen more than I talk; we can all connect with others and learn more about them. It's a question of asking great probing questions and being mindful about keeping the focus on the other person.

Before we get into the steps of how to hold mindful performance conversations, let's first look at the word "accountability" and how to create a team that is mindful of their responsibilities and keeps themselves accountable. Accountability is the basis of all performance conversations and must be fully understood before any progress is made toward a culture of mindful high performers.

CHAPTER 10

Accountability

The word accountability has

two parts:

Account +Ability = Accountability.

IN SIMPLE TERMS, ACCOUNTABILITY MEANS taking an account or recording the ability of ourselves and our people. People will demonstrate ability and the lack of it when completing daily tasks, duties, or interacting with customers. Some people have natural abilities. For example, an extrovert may have the ability to hold a conversation with anyone, but if you ask them to sell, they may not yet have the ability to perform that task successfully. A manager may have the ability to make a schedule but not have the ability to train people.

Everyone on your team shows different abilities or lack of them, which is a very positive thing. Hiring a team with diverse skills is excellent, and it allows us to have a "deep bench" of players who can tackle any task. The key is to synergize the various abilities within your team to work as one cohesive unit.

When we create a well-balanced team with different abilities who work well together, it creates our dream team. Even though each person on your team may show a different level of ability based on experience, personality, and knowledge, every person on the team must demonstrate a level of standards. This is where the ability to hold productive performance conversations helps hold team members accountable.

For example, if you were an Uber driver, you would have to show the ability to drive a car. All Uber drivers can drive a car, but how well they drive may vary. Some may interact with customers, and some may not. Some may be able to operate a stick shift, and some not. Some may even know the map of the city, while others would be lost without GPS. But at the end of the day, they must all be able to drive. They must show the ability to take a customer from point A to B and get them there safely. Let's apply this to a retail store. All team members must show the ability to interact with customers, work well together, and be on time for their shifts. This sounds simple, but not all employees successfully meet these basic requirements consistently.

This is where a manager's role becomes vitally important. They must assess and account for each person's abilities. Make sense?

So how do you hold people accountable?

It's an easy word to use, but not so easy to put into action. I bet if you asked ten leaders on your team what accountability means to them, they would give you ten different answers. Some may say writing people up, documenting performance, or holding a coaching conversation. Try it yourself. Ask your team what accountability means to them and see what they say. You will learn a lot about them as individuals based on their answers. And you will learn a lot about your organization as a whole.

Depending on your company and its structure for performance management, you will need to determine how to infuse a culture of accountability. But either way, it is every leader's job to create a culture of accountability, hold productive performance conversations, and deliver results.

Managers who build high-performing teams have mastered how to do this consistently; these managers get promoted faster.

Someone once told me, "When other people's performance starts becoming yours, it's time to take action." This was the best advice I was ever given in the area of accountability. It kept me objective and helped me realize the only job I had as a manager was to manage my team to the performance objectives and take action when they were not being met. When you think about it like that, it's an easy task. The key is to know what the objectives are, communicate them clearly and often, and measure how the team performs in light of those objectives.

How to Be Close, yet Distant

One of the obstacles to building accountability is becoming too personally close to the people you manage. When managers become too close to their teams, they can create considerable obstacles in holding objective performance conversations.

If this has ever happened to you, you will know what I mean. If it hasn't yet, then at some point it possibly will. This could hinder your career if you don't know how to get yourself out of these situations. It is said that we meet our best friends in retail. Working alongside people every day, getting to know them, pulls at our heartstrings, and it's easy to get personally involved. But what do you do when you have shared too much and need to put boundaries back in place? If you recognize that you or your employees have crossed the line, it is necessary to get back on track and manage your team's performance objectively.

There are specific steps that managers must follow to hold their team accountable:

- Understand each person's roles and responsibilities as per company guidelines.
- Validate and confirm that each member of the team understands their responsibilities.

- Set clear expectations with the end in mind.
- Give room for team members to develop the *how* (the steps toward achieving expectations).
- Focus on the results and what is expected.
- Provide consequences in advance. Avoid those "gotcha" conversations.
- Explain the impact of not taking action.
- Follow up and follow through.

Managers who put these steps in place set the stage for employees to perform at their maximum capacity and can hold their team members accountable and achieve higher results.

To be able to achieve all of this requires strong communication skills. It's all in the way that you communicate. It takes effort, skill, and practice. It also takes your commitment to making time for your people so that communication can happen.

Some managers think they have been clear but then wonder why things are not being executed as per company standards. If the standard you have set has not been met, it is either because you have not communicated it. Your employees don't have the desire to meet it, or they don't have the skills. All of these can be corrected through the last step in the ACT model. *Teach* and *mentor*.

But for now, let's assume you are doing all of this and want to proceed to a performance conversation. In the next chapter, we'll explore the power of conversation and how to use it effectively.

CHAPTER 11

Conversation is Key

A Life Lesson:

Words matter; choose your message with care.

HAVE YOU EVER BEEN IN a conversation where you kept getting disconnected? On FaceTime or an online chat, you know immediately when the call drops because, visually, you can see the disconnection. However, many people talk to each other all day long without knowing that there is a disconnect. There is no audible beep when humans lose their connection because they have failed in their attempts at communication.

Think about this for a moment: how often do you notice a drop in connection in a regular conversation? You probably won't if you're not looking for it.

In Les Giblin's Book, *Skill with People,* he states that you will become a better communicator when you understand people are only interested in themselves. This means most of us are preoccupied with ourselves in any given conversation. I have reflected on conversations where I didn't help the other person feel as valued as I could have due to this core human behavior. We all do it. When I teach listening to leaders in a workshop environment, we practice the art of asking a partner questions and paying attention to how many times we want to share our own stories based on what the other person is sharing. You see, this happens, like Les says, because of our preoccupation with self-interest. When someone else is talking, it triggers our memories and experiences, and we want to share them. This, however, does not build strong connections or help people feel valued. It actually creates a disconnect. If you want someone to feel valued and be known for being a great communicator, try this the next time you are in a conversation: Put your complete focus on the person you are talking with, and instead of sharing your experiences, try asking three probing questions to discover more about what they are sharing. As an introvert, this was my saving grace at social events. Because I am passionate about people feeling valued, I make it my mission to listen and pause my own life story when I am leading others.

I also think very carefully about what I say and how I say it. Words matter, tone matters, and being aware of how others feel during conversations is the leader's responsibility. Communication can break down when leaders are frustrated with their team members; even when you are frustrated, you should always be intentional about communicating in a way that helps your team feel valued. It sounds simple, but trust me when I say most issues stem from miscommunication.

Being intentional with communication takes paying attention to how often your focus returns to you and how you make others feel. The best leaders can see disconnections happening and quickly reconnect. This is something that I have always been good at; it is what makes people feel accepted, aka supported. When people feel heard and seen, they feel valued. I have spent my entire career helping others with this. And nine times out of ten, it comes back to the human desire to be right, be seen, and be heard. People want to be heard. If people wanted to listen as much as they wanted to be heard, we would all be more connected.

I try my best not to let frustration get the better of me. I focus on helping people feel valued, no matter what I have to communicate. Choosing your words wisely helps your team feel valued or not. Our communication as a leader shapes feelings and how others feel about themselves more than you know. Have you ever been in a meeting where you felt you wanted to say something but didn't out of fear that it would not add value to the conversation, or worse, that someone will judge you for your ideas? We have all had this experience. I know I have. If we know this, then as a leader, we must assume that others feel this way at some point.

With this assumption, our concern for valuing others would be amplified in how we respond to our employees at any given moment. Here are some examples of responses that evoke different emotions. See if you can choose which one would help your employees feel valued.

Employee: I am having issues this morning getting into my email. I can't follow up on things because it's not giving me access. I have a client that needs my help right now.

Wrong Responses

Manager:	Log out and log back in. Reset your password or ...
	Yeah, that happened to me last week. It's such a pain or ...
	It sounds pretty frustrating. I'm not sure what to do ...

These responses are neutral; they are not detracting; they are not adding value to the person. They are all focused on self—versus supporting the employee.

Correct Responses

> *Manager:*   It sounds like we need to help that client ASAP. Let's contact IT and see if they can help us get you back online right away.

This is a supportive response that will encourage the employee and create a positive emotional attractor.

> *Employee:*   I worked all weekend and missed my dad's birthday party.

Wrong Responses

> *Manager:*   Well, working in retail is hard. I worked through my best friend's wedding. That's how it goes.

This is all about the manager, no focus on the employee.

Correct Response

> *Manager:*   It sounds like this was an important day for you. Is it possible you can do something special with your dad this weekend? I'm sure your dad would love that. Let's make sure your schedule is set up so that your time is booked off.

There are clear connecting signals you should look for as a manager when you are communicating with your team to be sure you stay connected. Increased communication, particularly when there is a performance issue, fosters positive recognition, emotional bonding, positive energy, and growing synergy.

Let's assume that one of your employees is not meeting expectations in a specific area of responsibility. Every manager must review certain guidelines and behaviors before holding a performance conversation to help get the employee on track.

Provide Facts, Not Opinion-Based Feedback

Talking to an employee about vague, esoteric concerns or complaints is futile. Lobbing anonymous complaints at them just puts them on the defense. Instead, provide specific feedback, including factual examples that help to paint a picture.

Separate the Behavior from the Person

The actions of an employee should be the only subject of conversation. Personal attacks are unproductive and ineffective. Finger-pointing and "you" criticisms alienate employees. Instead, talk about how "we" can work together to address a performance concern. Assure your employee that you will give them the tools they need to succeed.

Demonstrate Empathy, Not Sympathy

Sympathy involves pity, and no one likes to be pitied. Sympathy creates emotional distance. Empathy requires a connection with a person's feelings as if they were your own. Sympathy says, "I'm sorry you feel that way." Empathy says, "I have felt that way many times myself."

Set Timelines for Improvement and
Explain What Progress Looks Like

Employees do not want to disappoint their managers. As human beings, we are wired to seek acceptance and approval. If you're going to give an employee a massive boost of confidence and commitment, spell out for him or her precisely what your expectations are. Then promise to provide regular feedback. Finally, set a date for when the employee will be reevaluated.

Set Your Employees Up for Success

Equip your employees to succeed by asking what the employee needs from you. Ensure you are clear it is the employee's responsibility to access the tools they need and put in the work necessary to improve. It is not your job to do their job.

Ask Them What They Will Do to
Improve the Situation

This is a great way to foster increased accountability. It also helps the employee to think about a performance weakness from a managerial perspective. Ask the employee what steps they believe will be effective at helping them to raise their level of engagement. Listen carefully to their answers, dispelling any preconceived notions.

Agree on the Next Steps

This is the most crucial step in the process. Make sure you and your employee are on the same page regarding the next steps. In so doing, you complete the cycle of conversation, and your employee walks away with a clear picture of what they need to do going forward.

So, now that you have the guidelines for performance conversations, how do you do it?

Holding mindful performance conversations is not easy, but the more you do it, the more confident you will become. They say that practice makes perfect, and you will never be able to predict exactly how a conversation will go—so, having some room for ambiguity is always good.

People are emotional, like we said earlier. There is a formula to have conversations that will usually leave the other person feeling good about the discussion. I've had people thank me in the past, as they had not been aware of what they were doing or how it affected the company or the team. I believe everyone wants to succeed. ACT—leading with awareness, having positive intent, and practicing mindfulness as a leader—when heading into these conversations. Staying close to the facts and staying unattached to the outcome will keep you in the driver's seat and help your employees feel supported. It will also keep you present, discussing the performance at hand, not what could happen, or getting derailed onto something else. Demonstrating mindfulness and bringing it back to the present moment is a skill and one that managers need to master to create the right conditions for their teams to thrive.

This applies in all situations when providing feedback, but even more so when you are preparing for a performance conversation that addresses an employee's abilities when it relates to not meeting the job responsibilities. You must have concrete facts, not opinions based on what you have witnessed this person exhibit.

This means you should not provide performance-based feedback based on what other team members are telling you. This can be a sticky situation for a manager.

How to handle these situations will not only create a culture of accountability but a high functioning team that works well together.

When preparing for performance conversations, you should reflect on the responsibilities and expectations you are asking of this employee. Once you have identified these, you must provide actual observed and factual feedback where the employee did not meet those expectations.

Using words such as "I feel like" and "I think you" are emotional statements and must be avoided. To turn this into a factual statement, it should sound like this: "Last week, we discussed the expectations about how to …"

"You agreed that next time you would …"

"You said you would complete as per company standard …"

"Today, I observed you …"

State What You Saw!

If an employee has been offered a plan to correct an issue but has not met his or her obligations, you might say:

- "This is what we agreed on. And this is what happened. Can you tell me why?"

- "Can you walk me through *what* you understand the expectation is?
- "Can you tell me *how* you intend to do things differently going forward?"

These are all great questions. An important consideration is to avoid getting stuck in the motion of over-coaching. This will put both of you in the context of, "Next time I will ..." The problem with that is when the next time comes, you will have to provide this coaching again and again. And guess what? Three months later, you may find yourself dealing with the same issues.

When you remind the employee you have already discussed the expectations, and they acknowledge it, the next question should be, "Help me understand *why* you are choosing not to do X?" This simple but effective question will put the ownership back on the employee and the current moment of what is happening. Do you see the difference? It makes the person you are asking think about what they do and why they choose to do it. It compels them to own the fact that they did not meet the expectations. Now, depending on the answer, you can decide where to go next. It puts the conversation in an ownership context.

Don't get stuck in the cycle of ongoing coaching and then walk away feeling you are back to square one, with no clear way of holding your team accountable.

This is what most managers do, unknowingly. Why? It's because we love to coach and help people. As retail leaders, we are trained to coach and love developing others. What about those instances when you are not present to witness an employee's behavior but hear about it from other employees or disgruntled customers?

This can happen to you, and it is your responsibility to address employee concerns and build positive cohesion in the team. Here is how you can handle this situation:

Let the employee who is sharing the information know you are listening and hear them, and reassure them you want everyone on the team to feel comfortable working together.

Gather the facts, not the opinions, by asking for specific examples and how it relates to job responsibilities and performance. Help them help you by asking for details based on tasks or duties that are not being met. This will help you provide fact-based feedback to your employees.

Addressing behaviors is always tricky for managers, especially if they are being brought to your attention by a team member who is having issues working with a colleague.

If you are not present when it's happening, you may not be able to witness or confirm the problem. This is why specifics are critical.

You need to be careful here. You mustn't become a dumping ground for venting, as this will not help the situation. It can break down teamwork and erode the positive, unified culture you have been working to build. My rule of thumb is that it needs to be relayed by three different people to ensure it is not just someone's personal bias towards another. You should always encourage team members to be open and provide feedback to each other. This builds strong teamwork. However, suppose you are in a situation where three different people have provided you with similar feedback on a team member, causing a breakdown in the roles and responsibilities. In that case, it will be your job to address the matter.

Here is some language you can use to tackle this delicate subject:

"Hi Sally, I want to touch base on a few things that have been brought to my attention. I think you may need some more training or support on ..."

This then allows you to move into the conversation by sharing facts, not opinions. Try to stay neutral with no judgment. Remember, you are there to help the employee receive feedback and understand what they are doing or not doing that is impacting the team. Help them acknowledge and set up the next steps with a measurable outcome. Remember to follow up and validate after the next shift to see how it went. Don't wait until several shifts later. It's important to schedule this follow-up for the very next shift. You may need to write this down in your planner to follow up. It matters to your team and can make or break teamwork.

Setting the conditions for performance conversations is just as critical as the actual dialogue. Sitting in the middle of the mall may not be the best place to hold a detailed performance conversation. This sounds like common sense, but I have sat in many food courts and overheard managers providing feedback which no one else should hear. So, find a quiet space and make sure you are not interrupted by the rest of the team or by customers, for that matter. Having high standards and helping your team members achieve their personal best is a manager's job. Sometimes, when it gets to the point of addressing more progressive performance issues, you will need to take a more structured step-by-step approach. This involves a progressive process that supports the employee's improvement and sustains positive performance.

Most organizations will have some performance plan or process in place. But where these plans fail is in supporting managers to prepare and execute. This is why many employees leave their jobs feeling they were not clear on what was expected of them or that their manager didn't like them.

The art of having employees resign on their own accord and helping them see that this may not be the right career choice starts with a two-way dialogue between the employee and their direct manager. This must be treated with respect. It is imperative to ensure the employee feels like they are being treated fairly. Even when the performance moves beyond a conversation to a formal process, it's still essential to follow the steps that we covered above.

There are five escalating steps in the process to manage underperformance, misconduct, and behavioral issues:

1. Diagnosing performance issues
2. Giving feedback
3. Performance improvement meeting
4. Documenting performance improvement
5. Follow up

Diagnosing Performance Issues

Once a performance issue is identified, the first step is to reflect on the situation and diagnose the root of the problem. Understanding the cause of the issue is the most critical component of addressing performance, as it will help you determine the next steps. If you don't address the cause your coaching and development of disciplinary action will not lead to sustained improvement. Diagnosing starts with the manager asking themselves key questions about the employee.

Giving Feedback

Once you have gathered the answers to these critical questions, it's time to decide what the next steps will be. The manager should now meet with the employee and take notes about the performance. The manager must be honest and provide strict expectations and an action plan to which the employee agrees. For this to be successful, it must be a joint decision. If it's a policy issue such as lateness, this needs immediate action from the employee; it's reasonable for you, the manager, to expect this and be clear about what will happen if the improvement is not seen immediately.

Performance Improvement Meeting

If an ongoing performance or conduct issue is unresolved, the next step is a formal meeting. You can learn all about this in our retailu course:

https://www.retailu.ca/course/the-five-steps-to-managing-performance

Documenting Performance Improvement

Immediately after this performance improvement meeting, the manager must document the meeting, including the date, time, and an outline of the discussion.

The easiest way to make a note is to write it like a script in point form or a brief overview. You do not need to make it a lengthy novel. Also, be careful not to put your opinions in your notes. Make it factual and concise.

Follow up

This is the critical last step. Following up to ensure everyone has the same understanding clarifies the path forward. An employee who understands and is willing to meet objectives will excel. Employees who don't may need to be let go.

CHAPTER 12

Building a dream team

A Life Lesson

*You are only as good as the team you
have built—so, build one that supersedes
your abilities and challenges you.*

TO LEAD A HIGH-PERFORMING RETAIL team and deliver exceptional results, attracting and retaining top talent is an essential leadership skill. The greater you are at recruiting great people, the further your career in retail can go. Trust me. I know this one very well from living it.

I learned a long time ago that resources like this book and retailu online training were essential in helping me train my team. Even though I have been leading teams for years, ongoing training enabled me to articulate to my team about leadership in a different way. Before reading books and becoming a Maxwell Coach, I could show people how to be a great leader by leading from example; but when I started to study leadership concepts, it changed how I communicated to my team. I was able to hold off-site meetings and utilize everything I had learned at a different level. John says if leadership is on a scale of one to ten, with ten being the highest, continually improving on the scale will help you attract and hire leaders on the top end of the scale. Every leader wants to work for a leader they can learn from, because leaders are learners. And if you're going to have a high-performing team of tens, then you had better be atwelve! Your leadership ability will determine the team that wants to work for you.

You will need to perform at your highest level if you lead a team of superstars. When I was a recruiter at Apple, I was fortunate to go to California for a recruitment training seminar. The training was fantastic and took us through Lominger Competency Hiring practices. We learned how to ask better questions and assess the answers. One of the things I remember the recruiters sharing with us was never to fall into the mindset, "They are not an Apple fit," when discussing a candidate. They said that there is no such thing as a perfect fit. There is only will and skill. The culture at Apple was that it was a diverse place to work, meaning that valuing a candidate's innate qualities is what drives their selection process. The recruiter shared some powerful examples. She said she was combing through the online applicants when she came across a cover letter that read:

> *It would be a dream come true for me to work at Apple. I have no qualifications or retail experience, but I just think I would be a great employee.*

She took a risk, set up an interview, and took a chance on this young gentleman, who previously had struggled with homelessness. He turned out to be a superstar because of his passion and desire. How many of us would have taken that chance and paused our judgment of his past? It was a great learning experience.

She also challenged us to look at the team we were hiring and place a mental image of the team on a wall. That way, we would ensure anyone we were adding to that team lifted the team and could be placed at the top of the wall.

We were asked to consider this every time we added a team member; we would place them at the top of the wall. As we continue to add highly talented people, it will eventually enhance the skills and abilities of the entire team. I always kept this in mind as I was hiring my director teams.

When you decide to build a team, you may inherit a team, be promoted within the same team, or have the privilege of opening a new location and hiring an entirely new team. Whatever the scenario is, being selective about the people you are adding, keeping someone on or exiting them off the team, can make such an impact that it should not be done without thoroughly thinking it through. Assessing talent is a combination of two things. It is the ability to use your gut instincts along with proven assessment tools.

I am the most optimistic person on my team, and because of this, it creates blind spots when I am assessing talent. I always ask others on my team to second-interview the candidates I am hiring for crucial roles. I am very self-aware that I may see the best in someone, hence the choice of relationships in my life.

As I say this, it makes me smile because of how self-aware I am. Like I said earlier in the ACT model, accepting your weaknesses is a good thing because when you accept what your abilities are and are not, you can get the right support to help you. Selecting the right people to add to your team is one of the most important decisions you will have to make. One bad hire can pull down the entire team dynamic.

I have made the wrong hires and exceptional hires. When you make a wrong hire, the one thing you can do is to take action fast and get them off your team. I have learned that if I am trying to convince myself why this person is great at what they do and am weighing out their value, they most likely should not be on the team. I learned my lesson here when I kept a manager too long. I kept thinking I could develop their skills. In hindsight, when I brought in another manager to replace them, the difference in the results and team were so dramatic I realized I should have made the decision a lot sooner for the sake of the rest of the team.

I have had the opportunity to work with top talent and lead extremely talented teams of people. It is one of the most rewarding jobs to lead a team of talented people who want to grow and learn. It is one of the highest callings and should feel like an honor every day.

If you are hired to lead a team, it will be vital you think through what your first thirty days will look like for the team. Why? Because, just like interacting with customers, first impressions matter. One of the most memorable moments I recall was when I was hired to be the regional director for Eastern Canada for DAVIDsTEA.

My first week at DAVIDsTEA included the district supervisor leadership conference, which meant I would meet my new team for the first time as a group. This was a bit nerve-racking. Generally, this wouldn't happen unless you lead a store team, where you are in the exact location every day. I wanted to make sure that I made a great connection with everyone, as most of them worked remotely, and this would most likely be the only time I would see them in person for at least a couple of months.

I decided to bring something to the conference that would be a great way to introduce myself and set the tone for the team in a fun and approachable manner. I remember reading in one of John C. Maxwell's books that someone once gifted him a specific type of notepad and how much it meant to him because of what was written inside. I thought this could be a great way to start the relationship with the team I was about to inherit. I had never given my team a gift like this before, but I knew I wanted to do something to set the tone and build trust from our first interactions. So, I bought my entire team a customized notepad. The notepad was not just a boring typical notepad. It was a notepad I customized on vistaprint.com.

On the front of the notepad, it said:

The greatest story ever told.

On the inside of the cover, it read:

Become the author of your story, create great
memories, say significant things, do significant things
and make a difference with people every day.

Fill this book with ... I make a difference stories
and I make a difference with other's stories.

This is the beginning of our story together October 2015.

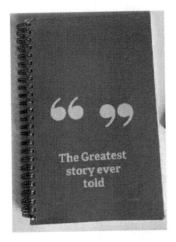

I presented each one of my team with their notepad. It was not a fancy notepad, but what mattered was the words printed on and inside. This was the tone I wanted our team to operate under. When I visited each leader, they were using them and were proud to share the stories about making a difference with their customers and store teams.

If you want to build a team, you need to think about what you want to be known for and find ways to motivate and engage your team members to help you.

Setting expectations is essential, as we discussed earlier in the book. But even more important is creating an environment where it inspires the people on your team to meet and exceed them. That day my team knew exactly what type of leader I was, and they made me proud, working hard to inspire their teams to make a difference. We won the Leger service award two years in a row and rated over 90 percent in customer satisfaction.

It is undoubtedly more difficult when you lead people remotely to make them feel part of a team. We had different strategies to encourage teamwork between the district managers. Some of them would work together and have peer-partner days. As teamwork was so important to us, they would encourage each other to switch districts and provide feedback on observed opportunities. This enabled them to have a fresh set of eyes in their stores. I think this was one of the most aligned teams I ever led. Everyone was in it for the team and for the company to win. So how do you build this kind of teamwork?

The best way to communicate the team's strengths is to share each person's strengths and passions with the entire team. Or, when members on your team come to you with ideas, ask them to partner with a particular team member who has the same passion or experience. This way, the team benefits and builds on concepts to make them even better. I did this quite often. Instead of providing all the answers, I would encourage my team to collaborate and share what they were working on individually and ask for feedback. Getting your team together to work on projects and training can be beneficial and is a great way to pull them out of their daily routines.

I would take my regional directors to each other's markets quarterly. We would visit stores, learn from each other, and spend quality time strategizing. We would end the day enjoying dinner together. By doing this, we would form strong relationships that benefitted the entire organization. If you lead remotely, this is important. Getting team members together helps them develop bonds and trust. Trust is the foundation of teamwork. Without trust, there is not teamwork.

Use the ACT leadership model when you are working with a team.

Accept: assess what is needed to build a strong team. When you accept reality and understand that it takes a group of multi-talented people with a different skill set than you and the team members to build a diverse team, you will be able to put a plan in place to add top talent and develop your team. When you lose judgment towards others, you can see beyond what comes naturally to you and ensure your team is well balanced. Putting a diverse team together is best for the team. Be aware of your personal biases.

Creating the team is the fun part. I developed a course on retailu called "Attracting and Developing Talent." You can use this information to help create the conditions and expectations to attract the talent you require. Invest time thinking about this. Remember what I shared about create? What you think about comes about. I had spent time thinking about what skills and abilities I would like to add to the team, and then miraculously the perfect candidate showed up in the form of referral or other means.

Teaching others is your job.

Coaching and mentorship is your most important job as a leader when you are building or developing a team.

Put ACT into action by following these simple steps, and you will be on your way to building the dream team!

CHAPTER 13

Agile Is the New Smart

A Life Lesson

Learning to accept and live in ambiguity is necessary.

BEFORE ANY CHANGE OF MINDFUL retail leadership can occur, the concept of evolution itself must be embraced. The world is changing at an alarming pace. We have seen the most significant communication shift the world has experienced in 500 years by introducing the internet and apps that keep us connected. The "neighborhood" has returned, but it has taken on a virtual form. People today have connections and access like no other generation. Retail leaders must adjust to the growing impact of technology and awareness among their teams.

The key to this adjustment is agility.

Agile leadership is a methodology that speaks to an organization's ability to change, adapt, and shift as the needs of the company, its employees, and its leaders evolve. Change is not feared in an agile leadership model; it is embraced, encouraged, expected, and welcomed. When change occurs, it does not frustrate the team; it motivates and electrifies them. It has been said that seven little words can kill any organization:

That's the way we've always done it.

Conversely, an agile team is always looking for and open to new ways to deliver higher levels of customer service and improve the corporate culture. Agile leaders know that their frontline retail workers are the key to agility in retail. Frontline employees know what doesn't work. And while they might not always know how to correct issues within the organization, they are excellent partners in finding creative solutions.

The benefits of agility in retail management are numerous.

Increased Employee Engagement

When employees know their feedback matters, they are more likely to give it. Furthermore, they are more inclined to be aware and think of solutions to be recognized for solving a recurring problem—the work environment shifts from one of struggle to a creative powerhouse of ideas. Employees have a stake in the success of the company. They help set the goals they are tasked with achieving. As a result, productivity skyrockets.

Increased Customer Service

As the organization streamlines, delivery to the customer improves. Employees enjoy greater flexibility allowing them to meet the end-users needs more effectively and efficiently.

Higher Quality Management

Retail managers can quickly develop tunnel vision and get lost in the minutia: Make the schedules, manage the inventory, and handle complaints. Agile leadership brings excitement back to retail. Rather than solving problems, managers guide employees on anticipating and avoiding them before they ever occur. Scheduling is no longer a nightmare when employees don't dread work and look for any excuse to take a day off.

Becoming an agile leader is the ability to navigate ambiguity.

I am the master at this. I think it is because I have moved to three countries, making me more resilient and open to new experiences. Sometimes it is hard for my team to accept living in ambiguity, as they like a plan, and I know that I can derail people because I can easily overuse this skill. Being self-aware and understanding where you overuse a skill in itself is a good quality of a leader, because then you can correct it or at least find ways to manage it.

When I worked at Apple, learning agility was the top core competency we looked for in candidates. The ability to learn quickly and adjust was essential for the sales team to replicate immediately. They required the ability to launch a product, learn with the customer, and become the expert, all in one day! I found this impressive. While working there in 2010, we launched the iPad. I watched nearly one hundred team members go into the launch of this product with little product knowledge, while maintaining the level of customer experience and service that Apple is renowned for. We asked questions through the interview process to uncovered learning agility, questions like:

"Tell me about a time you achieved something without having all the answers?" This is a great question to assess learning agility.

Another question, if you are interviewing leaders, could be: "What lesson have you learned that helped you change the way you lead?"

If you ask someone a question like this and they cannot answer it, it shows a lack of self-awareness and learning. Having agility means you grow and learn and apply. One of my biggest challenges is not overusing my leading with ambiguity. I have moved to many countries and love retail because it is forever changing; every day is different. This can create a lack of consistency in execution. Being an agile leader is a good thing; however, recognizing not everyone around you is as agile or positive about change is just as important.

Thinking through the impact of change on everyone around you is necessary. I have learned this working within operations. Providing specific direction, answers and mitigating the fear of the unknown is an excellent way to help your team be agile and move forwards.

I teach courses on how to build agility and raise tolerance of ambiguity for leaders through retailu. It is one of the competencies that leaders struggle with. I feel that today and in the future this will be the *top* competency and form of empathy required in retail management. We have seen the most changes in the past ten years, from mobile pay, ship-to-store, virtual try-on, and so much more innovation. To manage this, leaders need to deal with what they don't know more than what they do know.

CHAPTER 14

Collaboration—One Team, One Dream

A Life Lesson

Silos are real; break them by being aware
of how you contribute to them.

THE TERM, "ONE BAND, ONE sound," was made popular by the movie *Drumline*, in which a university marching band came together to win the most prominent band competition in the country. The term refers to joining multiple band sections (percussion, woodwinds, brass, dancers, and color guard) to create one cohesive and unified package.

The same is true for retail teams that want to deliver stellar customer service while preserving a positive employee experience. Perhaps in the retail world, we might call it "one team, one dream." The dream is to have happy customers who visit repeatedly and employees who feel gratified and fulfilled in their work. One great way to achieve that goal is collaboration. Collaboration between cross-functional teams creates healthy, functional, creative, and flexible corporate environments. Sadly, organizations can quickly spiral into a culture where battle lines are drawn between teams. Head office can easily be at odds with field leadership, and managers can miss the opportunity to interact with employees.

But a mindful leader who leads with awareness and utilizes the ACT principle understands that the most effective atmosphere is a win-win situation where people value the contribution of other teams to the organization's overall success.

A major issue in retail right now is how to align head office support functions with what the field operators want. They often think that they are on opposing teams and make assumptions about what other groups do, their value to the company, and their impact on their teams.

Retail managers at every level need to be empowered to make a difference. They can accomplish this when they know their function is related to all of the other teams in the company. One of the most significant "aha" moments in my leadership journey was when I learned to stop making these assumptions. As I transitioned from a field leader into an executive, my most significant learning was to stop assuming everyone in the office understood what and how to run a store.

When I was working in the field, I remember being overly anxious and too prepared for my head office visitors. We would clean for days before a visit, even paint walls, print new posters, order new mats, and all because a team from the office was coming to visit. We were fanatics about standards and presenting the store in the best possible light. I also remember the time I didn't prepare as much for a visit. This showed the reality of what a high-volume store on Saturday at two in the afternoon looks like during a massive promotion. After the second visit, we received more payroll hours and were given the tools and resources we needed to get the job done. Ensuring corporate visitors get to see the real picture is the way to go, this is difficult for field leaders to get right. As store teams want to put their best foot forward, and let their head office partners see the hard reality of leading a retail store.

It takes an entire support team to run a group of stores. However, I didn't view it that way in the beginning. My view was very narrow. I could not understand why some processes were implemented or decisions made. I would judge the teams who supported the stores and challenge the choices they made. As I transitioned into working alongside those business partners and put myself in their shoes, I quickly learned that they were trying their best to support and execute strategies that would help the business. There are so many challenges in retail today. It's tough, and every department is doing the best they can with what they know to develop creative ways to drive engagement and results. When I stopped making assumptions, took out the narrow view of perspective, and stepped into their shoes, it changed how I interacted and judged them.

Instead, I learned to understand my job is to support the head office partners and at the same time to support my team. This is a massive lesson for cross-functional teams in retail. When the focus is on collaboration and helping each other, the energy shifts, and lots can be accomplished. This means we must accept each other, appreciate each person's talents and abilities, and experience and work together for the better of the company. ACT, leading with awareness, can help build these bridges and form trusting valued relationships. This is easier said than done.

Silos Are Real

Teams are focused on their own objectives. Field leaders want more streamlined communication and less reaction to results. Those who provide support functions need to make decisions fast and change direction as needed to drive the results. Doing nothing is not an option, but doing something is. What should that something be, and how do you create collaboration across your organization to achieve results?

When practiced, I learned some key behaviors that can build help organizational health and break down the silo between field leadership and head office teams. Collaboration is key. What does this mean?

How do you practice it when all you can think about is, *What's wrong with that person? Why did they send that memo? Why did they make that decision?* For field leadership, it's essential to understand that your head office partners, in many cases, have not worked in a store and sometimes cannot be available as much as they would like.

It's important to work with your business partners and stop assuming they should know and understand what a day entails in the life of your job.

For head office leaders, it's essential to understand that your field leaders and team members have most likely never worked in your area of expertise and don't understand your challenges. They question everything you are doing, as they are the ones who have to execute and deliver on your vision. They wonder why some things take a long time to fix but others change rapidly for no reason, in their opinion. They sometimes have to answer questions from hundreds of employees without a full understanding of their decisions. These are two very different perspectives. It's essential to recognize that everyone is working towards the same goal: to please the customer.

Assuming positive intent, demonstrating empathy, and being curious should be human qualities every leader demonstrates.

I remember bringing a group of store managers into the office and sharing their day-to-day with the departments who asked them to execute their strategies. It was an exercise in building collaboration and positive intent. We completed a workshop that listed all tasks and the amount of time in a manager's week. These communications took them away from the customers and the sales floor. It was eye-opening! We then set up a goal with each department to reduce the duties and time taken to execute specific tasks. This was great, because instead of emailing a page of feedback comments, it created a relationship and human approach to this daunting task.

Each task was listed on a yellow post-it, and then, as we accomplished the task, the post-it was changed to pink. It was a great visual that helped us stay focused on streamlining the processes. Some tasks disappeared completely. There is nothing more frustrating for an operator than wasted time and productivity, especially when it doesn't positively impact sales. If you have never completed this exercise, I highly recommend it.

You can do this in any business. It helps you find time wasters, improve your productivity, and bring cross-functional teams together to collaborate. If you lead a store, a district, or a region, stop assuming your business partners are there to complicate things, and put your collaborative lens on. The next time you want to think to yourself, *Who came up with that idea?* change your thought to *Let's see how this works.* I mentioned earlier a great book called *Skill with People*, by Les Giblin. One of the chapters is about being an agreeable person and why this is important. The next chapter is about convincing people skillfully. He says that when you are an agreeable person and demonstrate this characteristic, others become more agreeable with you. This sounds counterintuitive. You may be wondering, *What if I don't agree with someone? What if I think what they say and do is not adding value?* He suggests that you can disagree. However, you should try agreeing for a short time to see what happens.

When you become agreeable, people like you. If cross-functional teams could demonstrate this powerful people skill more often, with a genuine concern and assume positive intent, teamwork would become stronger across all areas of the business.

When I started to understand its benefits, becoming more agreeable helped me achieve greater results, move the needle on more strategic initiatives, and build positive feelings between the office and the field operators.

To be more collaborative, there are some fundamental behaviors you can adopt in your leadership.

1. Slow down, say hello, and smile! This sounds so simple; but, when you have a million things on your to-do list, it's not always easy.

    When we smile at others, it is a scientifically proven fact that it causes others to smile. When we show kindness and others witness it, it is proven that those watching are more likely to act with kindness in the future. Kindness is something everyone can share, but we think of it as nothing. It is given through those who receive it and those who witness it. It is a source of power that, unlike other powers, can change the way others behave towards others and change their mental state.

2. Before making decisions, consider how people will feel. It does not mean that you must change your choice based on how people will feel, but it may give your perspective on how to communicate change, especially when it affects others. Be mindful of the bigger picture and how people's feelings can influence that. Our teams are the ones who deliver our message and initiatives every day to the customers; recognizing how they feel about what they do is essential.

3. Think about what you think about. The time we spend thinking about solutions versus the problems will serve our teams well. This is a big one; our team needs us to be resilient. Focusing on solutions and thinking about them creates resilience and helps instill this core competency in our people. Building a solution-based mindset across the different areas of the business will serve the entire organization well. These are easy ways to create a collaborative culture. We all want to work together to achieve the same goal: happy customers, happy employees, and a team that cross-functionally works together.

CHAPTER 15

Never Give Up

A Life Lesson

*Approach every setback with your own level
of awareness for contributing to it. Don't
blame others, even if it is tempting.*

TODAY'S BIGGEST HURDLE IS TO be agile, to streamline and remove the noise from the store level. With the amount of technology and pressure on bricks and mortar leaders to perform, execute, and manage, change happens rapidly. Whether you are a store manager, district manager, regional director, or executive, accept your responsibility towards building a collaborative culture across all business functions. This is not easy. It takes a commitment to activate this daily. Anything worth fighting for is not easy, and building resilience and change management into your leadership comes from experiencing it.

Think about the last time you had to decide without all of the information, or you had to execute something that you didn't agree with? Answer this honestly. How many conversations did you participate in that could be considered complaining? Be honest about how many people you affected (or infected) with your complaining. And how many complained to you? Next time this happens, what can you do differently?

When your team lacks trust in the organization you work for, how do you maintain and encourage people that it's going to be ok?

This is a tough one!

Retail is going through the biggest transformation I have seen in my entire career. Leaders who were once confident and delivered strong results are now questioning their abilities and doubting whether they have the skills necessary to make it. Conscious leaders are even more hypersensitive to the fact that their teams are looking to them to lead them through adversity. The conscious senior leaders I spend time chatting with are profoundly concerned and looking for ways to keep their teams engaged and motivated during the tough times in retail. Less mall traffic, fewer candidates applying, and higher wage demands compound the issues retailers are facing.

Back in the day, sales comps were everything. Our results measured us, and we took pride in delivering those numbers and winning the awards. I remember when I started to experience negative comps in my results and how that knocked my confidence. Before I relocated to Canada in 2006, I worked in Florida as a store manager in Banana Republic. The U.S. had experienced a loss in comp sales and lower traffic. The housing market was a disaster, and people had remortgaged to their detriment. Consumers had less disposable income, and they felt it. We did everything possible to try and improve the sales: restructuring, defining roles, offering discounts, and nothing seemed to work.

When I moved to Toronto, we were experiencing positive comps; Canada was performing well!

In 2008, we started to experience a loss in comp sales. I was still the same leader doing the same things that worked previously, but now I wasn't delivering. Why? Retail was changing, and the results were much harder to deliver. The conversion was still strong, but traffic was starting to decline year-on-year. Did it affect my confidence? Yes, no question. I am a results-driven leader. I have won awards and delivered positive results. So, what's the lesson here? I believe that during tough times you learn a lot more about yourself and your leadership. In a crisis or struggle, what is within you comes out. Just like when you squeeze oranges and juice comes out, being squeezed as a human can have the same effect, an outpouring of emotions

- I learned that even though my results were not always positive, my team was happy, customer satisfaction scores were high, and I had to dig deep to keep motivated to inspire the people around me.
- I learned that developing others became a way for me to feel successful, not the bonus at the end of the month.
- I learned that supporting my team, listening to my customers, and being a brand champion was more important than the numbers.
- I learned more about coaching, leading, and listening than I ever had and found other measures of success.
- I learned to control what I could and not worry about what I could not.
- I learned to find resilience in my leadership and how my energy and attitude affected others.

Why am I sharing this? Because I know that right now, there are leaders who have been successful like me, delivered the numbers and won awards like me, and have questioned their confidence like me.

It's a hard job at the top, and it's not always going to be easy. When you learn to trust yourself, develop others, and find resilience within your leadership, your teams and customers will benefit from it. The power of never giving up will inspire your team to do the same.

I know that it's hard to keep a brave face and smile all day when you feel like there's no hope. When this happens, do me a favor and think about something you can be grateful for.

Appreciate your gifts and remember the positive feedback you have received.

Find Ways to Celebrate Success:

- Internal promotions
- Happy customer stories
- Process improvement
- Retention of long-term staff

With every situation we are faced with, there is always something to be grateful for. Do something that will put you in a positive state of mind! When I was faced with a change in my personal life during my career, it would have been easy just to give up and say this is too hard. I was given the gene of never quitting, to which I am grateful, but that does not mean that it's been easy.

I recently had a conversation with my son, who told me, "Mum, you're always going to be successful." This made me smile, because he has so much faith in my ability to succeed and overcome adversity. I had to remind him that just because I make it look easy does not mean it is; I am human and have days where I doubt myself. I had a boss once who said to me, "April, you're like a pit bull dressed up like a fairy." At the time, I didn't know what he meant. But as I reflect on my ability to never give up, I know exactly what he meant by that.

Having persistence is not only a good leadership quality to nurture; it's a life quality that will improve your ability to succeed and overcome all the odds.

CHAPTER 16

The Right Culture

A Life Lesson

Don't underestimate the value of culture.
Listen when people speak; they know more
than you about their reality. If you are not
talking about culture, ask yourself why.

I TALKED WITH A COUPLE of girlfriends; one of them is an events coordinator for a multimillion-dollar beauty company. She complained that the company gave her an extremely small budget to pull two events together to promote a new line. "How do they expect me to accomplish this?" she wondered. Another girlfriend of mine then said, "Yes, and when you accomplish this, it will suck to be you because when you succeed, they will expect you to be able to do it again for less."

I pondered those words: "When you succeed, it will suck to be you." What a thought. But it's so true; when you succeed, more is required. I had to ask myself, *Does it suck, or is it a question of perspective?*

What culture have you created in your store, district, region, country, and company? Does it suck to achieve because you will be rewarded with a more cumbersome and impossible task? Or are results celebrated and truly appreciated?

Another girlfriend told me the company she works for had acquired another company, making them the biggest insurance company in the county. However, they made mistakes when blending the two organizations, even though they had gone through a merger just a few years earlier.

This brings up the question, Why? Did they not learn? The biggest question I find myself asking these days of companies and their leaders is: *Why* didn't they learn? You can answer this with many assumptions. Maybe there was a change in management, and nobody who was working back then is with the company today. Perhaps they are on autopilot and rolling out a plan that was already working. But clearly, they did not think through what they had learned. They hadn't tweaked the process. So, they crashed.

Did anyone in management think to ask the people working on the front lines or tenured employees what they had learned? Did anyone press the pause button long enough to consider this question? Probably not, because asking this question may bring up another list of tasks to start, and that would just take more time. Or maybe they didn't learn anything and will then have to admit to that.

A culture where no one is curious enough to ask the questions will produce major operational mistakes. Leaders can quickly lose sight of the process that leads to the result. When this happens, it means leaders have forgotten to listen. A better way is to stop, despite the deadlines and time constraints, and solicit conversation from the team.

Driving Culture

As a leader, we lead by example, demonstrating the three E's:

> *Engagement*

> *Emotion*

> *Experience*

As retailers become more experiential, employees need to provide customers with engagement, emotion, and experience. Retailers are changing the nature of the workforce. For example:

Best Buy has transformed the designation of its employees from "employee" to "tech consultant." Walmart has piloted programs such as offering personal shopping for online shoppers.

The goal of these innovative programs is to have highly engaged customers who are emotionally connected to the retailer because of high-quality customer experiences.

A Lesson on Perception

When I was promoted the first time as a director, my peers were asked if they wanted to work for me, and they all said no. I was surprised and slightly disappointed. When they were asked why, the answer was that I was self-centered, inflexible, and only out for myself. I was called highly competitive, and people were nervous about reporting to me, as they didn't see me as a caring leader. Getting this kind of feedback can be hard to swallow. If you want to build a strong team culture, it's not only necessary to have the respect of your direct reports and have them wanting to work for you. It's also important that your peers and cross-functional partners see you not as a threat but as a cooperative team player. Mine did not.

I asked them to give me the opportunity and provide me with feedback from the team anonymously through human resources after thirty, sixty, and ninety days in the role. This showed a willingness to change this perception and accept feedback rather than defend and justify my actions. My goal for those three months was for my new team to feel supported, valued, and heard. The focus was always on them and not on my agenda.

I was hopeful. I had positive feedback from the managers who previously reported to me. I was practicing leading with awareness, ACT. After the ninety days, the feedback came in, and it said things like, "She has done a 180," "She listens," and "I feel more supported than ever."

That was a tough time, being promoted internally and leading a team that was once my peer group; nevertheless, it was a great lesson in humility and perception. When you lead a team, it doesn't matter what you think of yourself; what matters is what they think of you. Perception as feedback was always tricky for me to receive, as I am logical and want to be recognized for the facts, not people's opinions. However, it was a good lesson learned. John C. Maxwell always says leadership is influence—nothing more, nothing less—which is true. It's hard to influence a team that does not like you. I learned a valuable lesson.

If you want the job, act as though you have it long before you get it. If I had thought like this, I would have worked harder on those perceptions being broken down before applying for the job. I would have built stronger relationships from the get-go. I remember a leader once told me that what everyone else thinks of you will either set you up for success or not, especially when you are promoted internally; she said you want everyone to say, "I understand why she got it."

Sometimes you need to accept where you are but not let the situation define you. Demonstrate, create, and think about what you want.

I was covering maternity leave as a temporary store manager in one of the highest volume stores in Miami. On my first day, I led six executive visitors through my store on one of the busiest days of the year, Black Friday. The visit went pretty well, I felt; I had finally made it to my dream job, managing my own store, even if it was temporary. Naturally, I always believed that people would recognize my work and then offer me more. In this case, they had offered me the experience of running a store through a peak period during the holidays. It was amazing, the team was awesome, and I rebuilt morale and hired an incredible team of people. Everything was going well when I saw the posting go up for the permanent store manager role on the company web page. At this point, I was confused, mad, and felt under-appreciated.

I went home and complained to my best friend and didn't know what to do. This was a big lesson in asking for what you want. I mustered up the nerve and asked the regional director to visit my store to share with him what we had achieved as a team. And let him know that I would not allow him to interview others for this store manager position and that I would be happy to accept it! He was pleased to offer me the position, and after this situation, I promised myself that I will always ask for what I want. The worst thing that can happen is that someone tells you no and why! I learned that nobody is a mind reader, and it's better to assume they don't know what you want unless you tell them. Too many times, we make assumptions that other leaders should know what we want, when they don't at all. This is not building an open and inviting culture; it is building quite the opposite. Fostering an environment where people are free to ask, share, and grow is difficult for most organizations.

I believe we can improve the culture of our retail community by igniting a global network of retail leaders who are leading with awareness and demonstrating ACT in their day-to-day behavior. We have the power to innovate the way people learn and lead. When we promote retail as a place to learn life skills, we open a vast array of opportunities for people to join our ranks. Retail is a place to be your best. We make retail a fun place to work and flourish. Happy people make happy teams and leaders. Retail is a fun career where, together, we can change the world.

It may seem ambitious to suggest that retail can impact the world. The truth is: it already does. More people work in the retail industry than any other. A retail manager touches many people's lives over their career, and those people reach many more; it's a ripple effect. Suppose we understand that we can inspire and challenge anyone to be a leader. In that case, we will commit to connecting with and empowering people to believe in themselves and the people around them. A career in retail is so much more than a job (or a first job). It is a proving ground, a place to cut one's teeth, and an environment where people can establish the building blocks that will shape their futures.

Retail leadership equals influence. That influence could be educational, confidence-boosting, and life-affirming if it focuses on building others. People end up in retail from many different avenues. Some people cannot afford to go to school to get educated and take retail jobs instead. Many students drop out then end up in retail to pay off debt and support themselves. Single mothers need a way to provide for their families. Often people rely on retail as a way to supplement another income.

The training people receive from a strong retail leader can empower and teach them management skills and ultimately lead them into jobs that become lifelong careers.

Being part of a winning team helps people feel valued and responsible. It teaches more than just selling clothes; it teaches us to connect to care, to listen, and to be kind—all human attributes that we require on this planet to save it.

Retail is much more than a part-time job. It's where you make a difference every day. I didn't go into retail as a conscious career choice; I did it out of necessity. I was faced at the young age of being kicked out of my house with good reason and finding a place to live and pay rent while buying food to feed myself.

I did what lots of young people do: I got a job in a retail store because I realized I had to drop out of college so I could pay the bills. I thought I would do this until I found a way to go back and finish school, which never happened. They say you meet your best friends in retail. I know this is certainly true for me. Last year on my birthday, for the first time I decided to invite to dinner twenty different people from different retail teams I had worked for over the past decade. This was a first for anyone who knows me—I rarely ever celebrate my birthday. Perhaps it's because I'm a twin, and it always felt weird to organize my birthday party.

Some people at the party knew each other, and others didn't, but the one thing they all had in common was retail. Whether they worked for Apple, the 'Bay, Mac, Holts, or had worked in retail previously in their lives, it was like sitting around a table with family.

And that's when I realized that they were my family—my retail family. Honestly, I could have invited more people, but I tried to keep it to a number that could sit comfortably around a table.

Even though everyone at the table had different roles in their retail career and different responsibilities, there was one thing every person around the table had in common, and that is our love of people. We all have the desire to help someone be better than they were yesterday. Developing others and relationship building is not for everyone. Still, these were probably the top two passions in life for everyone sitting around the table, and that's why we all ended up and stayed in retail in one shape or form.

Most retail employees feel like they work in a thankless job and are treated like it's a job for the uneducated.

If you love a challenge and have the drive to help others, you will love this undervalued career choice.

I remember early on in my career when I took on my first multi-site district manager role. I discovered that not every manager ran their store the same as I did. It was a big "aha" moment when I realized that my peer group did not lead their teams the same way, and it was now my role to align and empower them to make the best decisions for their store—I could not be present in every location every day. This was a huge lesson in trust, influence, and buy-in.

As I grew from district manager to director and then to vice president, one of my biggest focuses and challenges was never to lose sight of that lesson. I resolved to strive to create an empowered team who executed our strategies and the brand promise, down to the part-time employees in all two hundred fifty stores, even if they worked a four-hour shift and it was their third job. Many factors influence the consistency of your management ability to drive your customer experience. Usually it relies on 20 percent of the store employee population and managing communicating strategies to the rest of the population. This depends on many factors, but ultimately the team is only as empowered, engaged, and knowledgeable as the manager.

A manager's tenure and knowledge base will determine what they have to improve, train, and coach their teams.

Skill Levels of Managers Are Important

Are they organized?

Are they good communicators?

Are they good trainers?

Are they good at following up?

Are they great at inspiring and motivating the team?

Are they good at transferring the company strategies and knowledge to every person on their team?

Vacations, days off, and turnover are additional hurdles we have to overcome in retail management. Do managers have a successor to take on the communication piece and empower their team when taking time off? Is there a strong internal communication strategy or process to impart knowledge to the part-time employee from a 10,000-foot-high strategy?

I have often witnessed store team members say, "I'll call my manager for that," even though the manager is off. This has happened to me as a customer in the past. There's nothing worse than a customer not getting what they want and need, due to a lack of empowered associates who cannot make decisions on the spot. This impacts the customer's experience at that very moment.

Leading a team of regional directors and district managers along with 250 stores, I learned quite quickly that feedback could sometimes be filtered through people's own opinions and what they think the next level of leadership needs to hear. As it travels up to the office and executive team, the real honest feedback required to help change strategies and re-navigate the ship at large can get lost and softened due to a fear of sounding negative.

I know this as when I used to complete store visits, I would hear different feedback and ideas from the frontline staff versus asking my directors. I think it's because it is human nature that everyone wants to say the right thing. It is the responsibility of the senior leaders in any business to create a culture that is open and ready to listen, and then to take action on what is being shared.

When I was a store manager, I was coached on what to say and, more importantly, what not to say when I had executive visits. We need to empower the teams in an engaging way to build trust and engagement.

CONCLUSION

As I have said many times throughout this book, I have been fortunate to have great role models as leaders. I have worked for managers who cared about people more than about results. Sales are essential; there wouldn't be jobs without sales. But more than that, retail has brought people and opportunities into my life that may have never been possible in a traditional desk job. These experiences at the time felt like they were thrust upon me by circumstance rather than by choice. Looking back on them, everything that happened was with good reason and pushed me towards a leadership path that I did not know I was ready for or even aware of at that time.

That is why I founded retailu. I wanted to provide leaders with a place where essential concepts were defined so retail managers can grow. We:

- Teach people to lead.
- Teach people that their influence matters.
- Teach people how to prioritize people before business.
- Make retail fun.
- Make retail a rewarding career.
- Spark curiosity about the world we live in and of those we lead.
- Provide training to a global community of retail leaders in a way they understand.

Our business is people! So, every course we teach is designed to make learning to lead actionable. Retail is global; so is leadership, making them perfect companions. We want people in retail always to be curious, courageous, living to learn, and learning to lead.

Our ambition is to move retail from monotonous work to a vocation that has value, is meaningful, and gives people purpose.

Our training classes are designed for people who are just getting started in retail but would like to get a jump start on the path toward management.

In addition, we offer further courses designed for established leaders who just want to grow and develop their own skill sets. We have learning opportunities for everyone.

The retail industry is changing at an alarming rate. It is important to learn relevant skills to the global culture, so that you can always put your best foot forward and thrive rather than just survive!

The team is only as good as the leader leading them. This is what motivated me to start retailu to scale my knowledge and experience of leadership development and build high-performing leaders who drive high-performing and engaged teams.

Leaders lead. They filter and communicate priorities and focus on their teams. This creates teams that are connected to each other and to their customers. They can hear the voice of the customer because their managers hear their voices. This is role modeling ACT, leading with awareness at its best. When your team feels valued, guess what your customers do too. I achieved my success through leading with awareness and using ACT to empower my teams.

As my career grew, I had to develop my skills to meet the new challenges presented to me. As a result, I was able to create consistency of execution while adapting to changing demands on my abilities. To all the people I learned from, was challenged by, and are now called my retail family, this book is a reminder that anyone can make a difference in someone's life. I know because you have all made a difference in mine and mine in yours. When we do this, we inspire the human connection, which is a true blessing.

So, I leave you with this thought:

Be the type of energy that no matter where you go, you always add value to the spaces and lives around you.

Now that you have read this book, I hope that you gained some insights and lessons that can be applied. I am all about ACTion.

The ACT, the leading-with-awareness method of leading, is a way of being, which causes you to rethink how you live and lead.

Two ACTions for you to take immediately:

1. Head to https://www.retailucourses.ca/courses/the-positive-effect. These are *free* resources to help you put your new way of being into action. We have provided a cheat sheet with self-reflective questions to ask yourself daily, to check in and see how you are ACTing, along with a "How to Find your Purpose" six-page workbook.
2. Complete the following Start, Stop, Continue chart. This is meant to highlight to you how you want to take action.

What are my top takeaways from this book?

As I said, ACT, leading with awareness, is a way of being. Answer the following questions to have a positive effect on the lives of those you love and lead.

Start: What will I start doing?

Stop: What will I stop doing?

Continue: What will I continue doing?

Tools and resources to further your development.

My mission in life is to support you grow in your career, whether that be in retail or beyond, I absolutely love to develop leaders. This is why I've created more tools, resources and courses to support your personal development.

To learn more.

Check out www.aprilsabral.com where you can access free tools and resources to assist you in developing how to ACT and lead with awareness, along with purchasing my deck of inspiration cards and journal.

Check out www.retailu.ca for on-demand leadership competency online courses, workbooks, eBooks, and downloadable tools. Come join the retailu community.

Or get in touch with me directly at april@retailu.ca